ADVANCED MOTORING

ADVANCED MOTORING

An exposition of the basis
of advanced motoring
techniques compiled by the
Institute of Advanced Motorists
and with a Foreword by
the Minister of Transport

THE QUEEN ANNE PRESS LIMITED

WITH THE

INSTITUTE OF ADVANCED MOTORISTS

First published April 1967
Reprinted May 1967
Revised edition September 1969
Reprinted November 1969

Cloth edition   SBN 362 00002 6

Paper edition   SBN 362 00003 4

Published by The Queen Anne Press Ltd., St Giles House, 49/50
Poland Street, London W.1 and the Institute of Advanced Motorists
Ltd., Chiswick, London W.4 and printed for them in Great Britain
by Tonbridge Printers Limited, Shipbourne Road, Tonbridge, Kent

CONTENTS

FOREWORD

by the

MINISTER of TRANSPORT

There is no such thing as a driver who has nothing left to learn. Conditions are changing every day as more traffic comes on the roads. The skills learned ten or five years, or even one year, ago need continual updating.

To improve one's driving skill is not just a refinement of driving —it's a duty for every motorist. It's a duty which he owes to himself and his passengers and above all to other road users.

Unfortunately some drivers think they know it all. They are the danger. For though there are many ways of reducing road accidents one of the most effective is for motorists to drive better and behave better when driving.

INTRODUCTION

Practice, and the study of approved methods and techniques, are beneficial to *all* drivers in the interests of greater safety on the roads of today—and tomorrow.

This Manual is intended to give an insight into the manner whereby everyone, whatever may be their driving experience, can bring themselves up to the standard designated 'Advanced'. They may then, if they wish, enter for the driving test of the Institute of Advanced Motorists, which is widely recognised as being a criterion of good, safe driving. Even if they do not pass it, they will receive some valuable advice as to why they have failed.

The Test is conducted by Examiners drawn from the ranks of the Mobile Police, each of whom is the holder of the highest Police Driving Certificate and has been selected for duty with the Institute by virtue of his ability to assess whether a candidate drives with the skill and responsibility required by I.A.M. standards.

They act under the direction of a Council on which sit representatives of distinguished bodies in the fields of Road Safety, Medicine and the Judiciary, as well as Members of Parliament and noted personalities in the motoring world—all of whose services are entirely honorary.

The Institute of Advanced Motorists, founded in 1956, is a non-profit-making body, and has as its main objective the improvement in standards of driving and the promotion of road safety. Fuller information about it will be found at the end of this Manual.

Chairman, Institute of Advanced Motorists

TESTING   TIMES

The driving licence was introduced in 1904.

Anyone turned 16 (14 for motor-cyclists) with five shillings till then had the right to buy one over the counter, after filling in a form in exactly the same way as a dog licence.

A growing motor vehicle population in the early 1930s made it desirable to test new drivers before a licence was issued.

As from January 1st, 1935, therefore, an official driving test became compulsory.

Holders of licences issued before that date retained the right to renew them automatically, and this still applies.

Many drivers of middle, and advanced, age on the road today have, accordingly, never taken the official test.

Holders of current licences who have not driven a car for years, or passed the test, are thus legally qualified to do so.

The L-test, conducted by the Ministry of Transport's staff of Examiners, is designed to make a candidate prove his ability to drive with a set standard of competence.

He must also demonstrate having a sufficient knowledge of the Highway Code.

The legal requirements concerning the vehicle itself are laid down in 'Construction and Use Orders' made under the Road Traffic Act.

Trafficators of a mechanical or electrical nature are liable to suffer breakdown. Hence the Ministry's Examiners insist on candidates understanding, and giving during the L-test, arm signals as specified in the Highway Code.

Having passed the L-test, and being given the freedom of the road, a driver may renew his driving licence indefinitely, subject only to being able truthfully to sign the required declaration as to bodily fitness.

He should, however, realise that this does not automatically make him an expert driver.

I

'ADVANCED' DRIVING AND WHAT IT IS

IT ought to be the aim of everyone who drives a motor vehicle to have the will and the skill to keep clear of avoidable accidents.

Whoever takes pride in driving should be willing to accept the premise that there is a correct method of carrying out every manoeuvre.

An 'advanced driver' is not a racing or rally driver. Neither is he a 'slowcoach' in the obstructive sense.

He is a safe and competent driver whose passengers enjoy riding with him because he does not frighten them by taking risks or being ill-mannered towards other road users.

How does an advanced driver differ from one who has just passed the L-test? Although the latter has achieved something, it simply means that he is officially considered capable of handling a motor vehicle on the public highway unaccompanied.

Once this first and important hurdle has been cleared, experience can be gained and education in the real 'art' of driving can begin. The intermediate or Grammar School standard will be reached with practice.

In this book we shall talk about the many facets of driving and the meaning of 'planned systematic' driving, which is another way of describing advanced driving.

Study as well as more practice are needed to make perfect in this, as with all other arts. Just as you would not claim to be a surgeon because you can carve the Sunday joint, so passing the

L-test does not mean that you have automatically become a first-class driver.

Good driving has been defined, and correctly, as being on the correct part of the road, in the gear best suited to immediate future requirements, and travelling at a speed consistent with prevailing conditions and general safety.

Advanced driving means all that—and a little more. You must drive with not only skill but with responsibility—responsibility towards every other road user, including pedestrians.

The word responsibility is important. It means that you will *conduct* your vehicle, using that word in the French sense ('un conducteur'=a driver). It signifies something indefinably more than merely sitting in the driving seat and making the 'thing' go.

We have, indeed, no exact translation for 'conducting', exactly as with the French word 'circulation', which does not just signify traffic but the ability of traffic to flow freely. Or, again, for that old familiar 'chauffeur', which in literal translation means 'warmer-upper'.

To date the best qualifying adjective the English language has evolved for a really good 'conducteur' is 'advanced driver', indicating technical skill to control a vehicle expertly, and responsibility in the manner that skill is exercised.

Physical and mental fitness also enter into the make-up of an advanced driver. He should not suffer other road users to be put in jeopardy through liability of his physique to sudden blackouts, or to the ill-effects of defective vision.

Neither will he allow business or domestic worries, or some temporary physical unfitness, to interfere with his concentration while at the wheel. Whilst he is driving he regards it as a whole-time job.

The major cause of accidents is human error. We *all* make mistakes, and the infallible driver has not yet been born. But the endangering of others besides ourselves by taking an unnecessary risk is unforgivable.

II

VALUE OF GOOD INSTRUCTION

IF every motorist drove skilfully and responsibly, there would be little need for arbitrary speed limits and many of the irksome restrictions made necessary by an irresponsible minority.

Criticism is often heard about the official driving test—is it difficult enough, should there be testing on icy roads or in darkness, snow or fog?

Were the authorities to act on these remarks, a learner driver would have to wait a very long time to get a test or retest, for climatic conditions cannot be produced to order, and during the summer months nights are short.

Passing the L-test merely marks the end of the beginning of a driver's education. It only implies that the Examiner considers the candidate safe to take his car unaccompanied on the road.

After it comes the time when the real 'art' of driving should be studied. No matter how long you drive, you will never cease to learn something fresh about the behaviour of motor cars and the people who drive them.

It cannot be too often repeated that 'Accidents are caused— they do not just happen'. The majority result from human error.

But the driver is not necessarily the invariable culprit— pedestrians, cyclists, motorcyclists, and moped riders can do foolish things which precipitate accidents.

Proper education on the dangers of the road can do much to help. Casualties to children have been kept in check by safety lessons given at schools.

All police drivers have to go to school to become the experts they are. Accidents to their cars have been drastically reduced since the police driving schools were started.

There is no substitute for good instruction, and with the right basic instruction the average enthusiastic young man or woman who wants to become a good driver can do so.

But there is no short cut to that desirable end, and a 'Do-It-Yourself' advanced driving kit does not, and never will, exist.

If you watch a first-class batsman playing against a fast bowler, the thing that may impress you is that he always appears to have time to play his stroke to best advantage.

Similarly, if you watch a front-rank motor-racing driver you will notice that he is never hurried but that his every action is deliberate and planned.

This is the result of natural aptitude—but combined with hours and hours of hard practice.

Few ordinary drivers, however, trouble to force themselves to take intelligent practice once they have passed the L-test. If asked why, many will talk about the cost of petrol.

Compared with the cost of an accident, the cost of petrol is infinitesimal.

A driver cannot be the complete master of his machine until he knows with reasonable accuracy exactly how it will behave under all circumstances.

He should be fully aware of its acceleration and braking potential and be able to handle its gears and clutch capably. In the case of a car with automatic transmission he should so control the accelerator that the gears change themselves without jerking the car.

Where a manual-change gearbox is fitted which is without synchromesh, he should learn how to double-declutch so that a smooth change up or down is obtained, from any gear to any other one, with the car moving.

Since brakes are not infallible, their failure to act under emergency conditions could produce accident conditions, which might be minimised by engaging low gear.

Nothing could be worse for a driver than to be faced with the prospect of his vehicle running away on a hill because he lacked the necessary skill to mitigate the possible effects by thus utilising the engine and handbrake to maximum effect.

III

SMOOTHLY AND SAFELY

Now, in the minds of many people the term 'advanced driving' is synonymous with driving at high speeds. This is quite mistaken.

Advanced driving, we repeat, should imply smooth, safe progress, being on the right part of the road in the correct gear and travelling at a speed consistent with safety and prevailing conditions.

If all drivers would follow this precept the roads would be safer for everyone. The limit of one's speed should be the range of one's vision.

While speed of itself is not necessarily dangerous, if indulged in at the wrong time and in the wrong place, with the wrong hands in control it most certainly is.

There is a wide gulf between speed properly used and speed which creates danger for other road users.

The laws relating to motoring offences differentiate between exceeding a speed limit and driving at a 'speed dangerous'.

Driving a car on the public highway (or motorway) is a privilege and not a divine right—a privilege which carries with it the paramount responsibility of not endangering others.

Although the infallible driver does not exist, and everyone is liable to commit an error of judgment, we *can* avoid taking unnecessary risks. A learned judge once said: 'Before making any manoeuvre with a motor car, first make sure that it is safe to do so'.

No sounder advice than that could possibly be given.

Whenever you are planning a long-ish journey by car allow for unexpected hold-ups. Never let your driving degenerate into a race against the clock—or against others.

The competitive spirit, which makes some drivers resent being overtaken and engenders a burning desire to show the other fellow 'where he gets off', is a prime cause of accidents.

Maybe pride of ownership spurs the driver of a family saloon to try to demonstrate that it is just as fast as the other chap's and take foolish risks after being overtaken.

The enquiry 'Did you have a nice journey?' often brings the reply: 'We did X to Y in two hours—that's an average of Z miles an hour'. But to find out whether this was an example of good driving you should ask the passengers if *they* enjoyed the trip.

Drivers who scare their passengers are either bad or plain ill-mannered—perhaps both. An advanced driver is always mindful of his passengers' comfort and peace of mind, and of their safety.

IV

'READING' THE ROAD

D RIVING demands not only concentration, but observation and intelligent anticipation. In some ways it is like a game of detection—searching for and interpreting clues—and this means reading the road like a book.

It is amazing how skilful one can become at this with practice, and what tremendous satisfaction one can derive from saving others from the folly of their own actions.

Good vision is the first essential. Always start a journey with the windscreen and windows clean. Iced-up or misted glass is a menace to safe driving. The rear view mirror should always be checked before starting and adjusted so as to reflect the fullest possible picture of the road behind.

At first moving off, particular attention must inevitably be paid to the immediate surroundings. As speed increases the driver should raise his sights to focus observation mainly further ahead.

Watch out for changes in road surface so that well before reaching perhaps potholed or skiddy-looking sections the speed of the car is adjusted to suit.

Develop the knack of spotting warning signs long before they are reached and be fully conversant with the meaning of symbols and of advance direction indicators.

Be prepared to cope with the child, elderly person or even dog taking a sudden fancy to cross the road, or a cyclist who may wobble or swerve without warning.

Anticipate the emergence of someone from behind a stationary vehicle by looking for feet showing under it while still some distance away.

A puff of smoke from the exhaust pipe of a parked vehicle will indicate that it may suddenly start to move. A reflection in a shop window at a street junction will often reveal whether another vehicle is approaching. Passengers walking towards the rear platform of a moving bus give an indication as to whether it is about to stop—and the conductor's hand raised to ring the bell that it is going to move off.

Wheel tracks or mud dropped from farm vehicles in country lanes warn of hidden entrances or gateways. So, too, do shadows which indicate whether a gate is open or closed, or gaps in hedges through which animals might wander. Approaching a lane junction, these gaps can be used to advantage to observe vehicles coming from the right or left.

Tradesmen's vans standing opposite isolated cottages warn that the milkman or baker might suddenly dash across the road to pick up further supplies. Great care should be taken when approaching ice-cream sellers near schools to avert danger from children dashing suddenly into the road.

Telegraph wires can indicate the sharpness of a bend, but this is one clue which should not be interpreted too literally, as they sometimes veer off the road into fields.

If two dogs are approaching one another on opposite sides of the road there is every likelihood that one of them will dart across.

These are some of the 'letters' in an advanced motorist's alphabet which enable him to 'read' the road ahead. By continuous practice he learns to forecast the actions of other road users, even animals, and to be forewarned against emergencies. He covers his footbrake pedal with his foot at the first sign of danger. This could reduce his overall thinking and braking distance by at least 22 feet from 30 m.p.h.

V

PLANNING YOUR DRIVING

As we have said, good driving really amounts to being 'on the right part of the road, with the correct gear engaged and travelling at a speed consistent with safety and prevailing conditions', **at all times.**

The first and last of these factors are so obvious as to require no further explanation, but the importance of 'the correct gear' is not always appreciated.

There are three primary means of dealing with an emergency: one is to steer away from it, another is to try to avoid it by braking, while the third is to accelerate—and it is often possible to accelerate out of danger, whereas to brake would mean stopping right in front of it.

But remember, you have good acceleration **only** when your engine is pulling in the right gear.

To know whether you are in the right gear, get in the habit of asking yourself as you drive: 'If I were to press the accelerator at this precise moment, would my speed increase rapidly enough to get me out of trouble in an emergency, or would the engine fail to respond?'

The real art of driving is based on what is known as 'planned systematic car control': if you learn this thoroughly and apply it consistently it will become instinctive.

Then, your driving difficulties will disappear because you will arrive at all hazards on the right part of the road, in the correct gear, and at the right speed.

There will only be one job to do with your hands—to turn the steering wheel; and one to do with your feet—accelerate or brake.

It should not be difficult for the average intelligent person to apply his or her natural instinct for planning to the job of driving.

By employing our system you will eliminate most driving faults, including that very common one of releasing the steering wheel with both hands whilst changing gear and signalling, all simultaneously.

To learn to plan you should imitate the air pilot's drill—remember the initial letters of a series of operations.

Here they are for a car:—C.M.S.B.G.A.

The letters represent the words: Course, Mirror, Signal, Brake, Gear, Accelerator.

A simple code to assist you in remembering the sequence is the sentence 'Can My Safety Be Given Away'.

This is how to put the drill into practice:

C Mentally select the correct *Course*. If you intend to go straight ahead, this will be the centre traffic lane if there are three: the nearside one if there are two. If turning to the right, stop with the offside wheels just inside the centre line. If going to the left, keep to the nearside.

M The rear view *Mirror(s)* should always be checked before changing course, or even altering speed. And don't forget that there is usually a blind spot on the rear offside quarter of a car body which an interior mirror fails to show.

S Give the appropriate *Signal, clearly and in good time, before* taking up any course which involves a deviation from a straight ahead path.

B Apply the *Brake* whilst the car is travelling on a straight course, to bring the car's speed down to one appropriate for changing into the correct gear for negotiating any approaching hazard, such as a turn to the right.

G Change into the correct *Gear*, and again check following traffic in your mirror(s) just in case someone is attempting to overtake you in spite of your precautions. (Note.—The gear selected will depend on traffic conditions and the speed at which the particular hazard can be negotiated with complete safety. This must rest with the driver, and be consistent with the conditions prevailing and immediately to follow.)

A The only thing now remaining to do is to apply *Acceleration* correctly. Depending on road conditions, the most likely place for a skid would be when you are turning, so, if the road is wet, greasy, loose, or liable in any way to encourage skidding, keep the car under very gentle acceleration as you round the turn and apply firm progressive acceleration only when once more travelling on a straight course. On a firm, dry road you can apply progressive acceleration as you make the turn.

A breakdown of accident figures reveals that a very large proportion occur when turning right. The majority could have been avoided by exercising reasonable care, and by following this golden rule: 'Always pass round the back of oncoming traffic—never cut across the front of it.'

It is extremely difficult accurately to assess the speed of an approaching vehicle, and in any case the time saved is not worth the risk involved.

Admittedly, there are crossroads which are not an exact +, also other kinds where the 'golden rule' is difficult to apply. In such cases you can adopt the alternative of giving way to an approaching vehicle, or proceeding if he gives way.

Sometimes another driver will *force* you into making a nearside-to-nearside turn; when this happens, be very careful indeed of traffic coming from your left, as you could so easily be held to be in the wrong.

Planned systematic driving can be applied to any and every hazard on the road, and for this purpose 'hazard' means anything which could cause you to change course or alter speed.

VI

THE TECHNIQUE OF STEERING

THE quality of a driver can be judged, among other things, by his deportment at the wheel.

The 'great relaxed' is a common type, who slouches over the wheel, nonchalantly holding a spoke with two fingers of one hand and with elbow resting on the doorledge. Give him a wide berth—either he will do the wrong thing in an emergency or he may fail to gain control until it is too late.

The best drivers hold the wheel with their hands at the 'ten minutes to two' or 'a quarter to the three o'clock' position. If the seat is properly adjusted your hands will fall naturally into one of these positions.

Either hold will give you a wide swing in an emergency, without having to change the position of your hands.

When turning the wheel, use a push-and-pull movement; it is best not to let either hand pass the 'twelve o'clock' position when you are in forward motion. (This does not apply when reversing or manoeuvring in a confined space.)

If you are negotiating a slight left-hand bend, requiring only a quarter turn, raise the left hand to twelve o'clock and pull the wheel down, letting it slide through the right hand.

In this way you will find that both hands are opposite each other at the apex or most dangerous part of the bend, and perfectly placed to apply correction or take evasive action.

To apply full lock for a right or left turn, raise the appropriate hand to twelve o'clock and pull the wheel down to its maximum extent, at the same time sliding the other hand down to take over and push the wheel up to the twelve o'clock position again, repeating as necessary.

Having completed the turn, feed the wheel back again in the same manner. Do not permit it to self-centre unchecked.

Whenever driving technique is discussed, we are reminded that some racing or rally drivers use a different method.

Driving on the road and driving on a race track are two entirely different subjects.

This book is intended for the everyday motorist; there are others written on the subject of racing.

The fact is that what is permissible on a track could be suicidal on the public highway.

Hold the wheel firmly but lightly, so that you can 'feel' all movement. Tighten your grip only for cornering or fast driving. Avoid a vice-like grip; it is tiring and creates harsh movement, which is one cause of skidding.

Also avoid swinging in or out when overtaking. Make all deviations gradual, because stability deteriorates when a car is driven in a curved path.

Steer to fine limits only when you are obliged to do so by traffic conditions. At all other times leave a reasonably wide margin for safety; for instance, a door might open without warning on a stationary vehicle, or a pedestrian run from behind it.

Avoid steering for long periods with one hand only on the wheel. Never, under any circumstances, take both hands off when the car is in motion.

The steering of your particular car may be light, heavy, high-geared or low-geared. It may have a tendency to 'oversteer' or 'understeer'.

The important thing is that you have the ability to recognise and adapt yourself to any particular characteristic.

But don't let your imagination wander to the extent of blaming

26

the car for a steering fault which was really on the part of the driver.

If you don't understand technical jargon, the simplest explanation of oversteer and understeer is 'Oversteer, when the car is *more* anxious to get round the corner than is the driver—Understeer, when the car is *less* anxious, etc.'

When you change your car, get to know the new one's characteristics thoroughly, i.e., how does it steer, brake, accelerate?

Find the most comfortable seating position, learn all about the new controls (the trafficator switch on your last car might be the overdrive on this one).

Many of us spend a great deal of time in a motorcar, so it is worthwhile taking a lot of trouble to make our driving position comfortable.

This may even entail moving the seat runners, or, better still, having them moved before taking delivery. Discomfort increases driver fatigue, and there is a danger in fatigue.

Many cars have a driving seat with a good range of adjustment, but too few have seats which can quickly be adjusted to suit both husband and wife.

This may result in the dangerous habit of padding out with cushions, which can slip at the crucial moment.

If your driving seat cannot be taken forward sufficiently to enable you to reach the pedals in comfort, there are backrests on the market which will remain firmly in position.

VII

USING THE BRAKES

THERE is much more to braking than merely applying pressure with the foot to a pedal. Good braking is an art which is acquired only by practice and experience.

Brakes should be applied smoothly and progressively for approximately two-thirds of the distance in which you wish to bring the car to a normal stop, and the pressure gradually released for the remaining one-third.

This will allow you a margin for error of judgment or for re-applying pressure in an emergency.

To stop the car without the slightest jolt, release the brakes entirely during the last few inches of stopping.

This requires a considerable amount of practice, but you will be amply rewarded when your passenger looks up from his book and remarks 'Oh, I didn't feel you stop'.

Braking at speed can be a hazardous business, and should invariably be applied in time to take alternative action in the event of failure.

Always take careful note of following traffic before applying the brakes. If you are followed by what appears to be a good roadworthy car, keeping at a safe distance from your rear bumper, normal braking is adequate. If, on the other hand, you are followed by a dilapidated 'banger' – probably too close for comfort – you have two dangers to deal with; an unsafe driver and unsafe car. One way to avoid an infuriating rear-end collision in this case is to bring your braking lights on when you think *he* should commence to brake!

This should also be remembered when you are following another vehicle which may have more efficient brakes than your own. Always keep at a safe distance, of the order of about one yard per mile an hour. When travelling at 30 miles an hour you are covering 44 feet per second.

Three times any given speed calls for nine times the braking distance. It is imperative that allowance should be made for this fact of motoring life.

Brake only when the car is travelling on a straight ahead course. When rounding a bend centrifugal force causes extra weight to be thrown on the outside of the car. If you turn to the left you will feel it go down on the right, and vice versa.

Also, the front wheels exert the strongest retardation with modern braking systems and so the extra weight on the outside front wheel is intensified.

This could cause the car to use it as a pivot, and it will depend on your speed at the time whether the result is a serious accident or merely that you are badly scared.

When travelling at slow speeds and under normal road conditions, this effect is of course much less because there is little or no weight transference, but even so it is not good practice to brake on a bend or corner.

Even the efficiency of a first-class braking system which equalises force on all wheels will be reduced if uneven tyre wear or pressure is permitted.

Brakes stop the wheels, but it is the tyres that stop the car. Bald tyres may stop the car reasonably well on dry, firm surfaces, but not when the road is wet. Running on bald tyres is dangerous economy, and against the law.

Braking distances therefore depend on many factors. Your pressure on the brake pedal must vary accordingly. And remember that fierce braking, which may lock the wheels at 30 miles an hour, costs perhaps one month's normal tyre wear. Bad driving is not only dangerous but expensive, and locked wheels don't stop the car as well as wheels on the point of locking.

VIII

DEVELOPING ACCELERATION SENSE

Acceleration sense is one of the most important aspects of good driving. It is not possessed by every driver, and lack of it undoubtedly is the cause of accidents.

When we talk of acceleration sense we mean many things: the ability to judge the speed of one's own car in relation to that of the vehicle to be overtaken, and also the speed of any following or approaching vehicle, plus the acceleration potential on each of your gears.

Admittedly it is difficult to gauge the speed of an approaching vehicle, and even more so of one that is coming up behind.

But we can keep out of trouble if we follow the advice given in the Highway Code: 'If in doubt—do not overtake'.

Continuous practice in estimating the exact spot where you will overtake a vehicle ahead or pass an oncoming one, or where a following vehicle will overtake you, is an invaluable aid to carrying out such manoeuvres with safety.

Your skill in speed judging, however, should not encourage you to overtake in the face of oncoming traffic with inches only to spare, because engines do occasionally hesitate, worn tyres burst or drivers swerve or change course without apparent reason.

A really first-class driver may drive fast, but he does not take risks. Speed of itself is not necessarily dangerous, as we have said, but at the wrong time or place it is responsible for many serious accidents.

The criterion for speed is always that it is consistent with safety—your own and that of others—and prevailing conditions. During the lifetime of most of us, the speed of the ordinary car has doubled—trebled in many cases. Cars capable of one hundred and fifty miles an hour are to be bought, and this speed means 220 feet per second.

On a fast car the accelerator should be regarded as an instrument, not merely a pedal, and as such used with delicacy and precision.

Acceleration should be achieved progressively; whether gently or firmly must depend on road conditions, and should vary as changing surfaces and conditions are met with.

Stabbing on the accelerator causes waste of petrol and a lot of unnecessary noise. Excessive acceleration, which spins the driving wheels when starting away, proves only two things— bad driving and a desire to 'show off'.

Intelligent use of the accelerator coupled with observation and anticipation reduces braking to a minimum and saves unnecessary wear and tear.

It is a well known fact that two drivers using the same car will achieve very different figures for petrol consumption. The heavy-footed type who leaves everyone standing at the traffic lights, who overtakes you with a roaring engine and his accelerator pressed down to the boards, will probably get 20 miles per gallon against a good driver's 30 or perhaps more.

Anyone can drive fast, but to drive fast **with safety** is an art. It is possessed by some, who have usually acquired it through painstaking experience. They always remember that the accelerator is an excellent servant but a very dangerous master.

IX

ROUND THE BEND

A CCIDENTS which result from 'running out of road', or overtaking on a bend, are inexcusable and caused only by rank bad driving.

In all matters connected with driving, 'attitude' is as important as aptitude. The criterion for dealing with bends and corners should be 'how safe?' and not 'how fast?'

Centrifugal force is a natural phenomenon which has an important effect on driving. It is easily demonstrated, as follows;

If you tie a weight on to a piece of string and swing it in a circle, the weight will exert a pull on the string. This pull-away from the centre of the circle is called centrifugal force.

If the speed at which the weight goes round is increased, a point will be reached where the string snaps, and the weight will fly off on a tangent to the circle.

Similarly, if your car's speed is too high when taking a bend, centrifugal force can reach a stage where it will 'snap' the grip of the tyres on the road.

The car, like the weight, will go careering off at a tangent, and probably with very unpleasant results.

Now, racing drivers have a saying in connection with bends and corners: 'in slow, out fast'.

It is their superb skill in assessing a bend, taking the correct line through it, in the correct gear and at exactly the right speed, that enables them to maintain a high speed and at the same time reduce risks of 'snapping' to a minimum.

They would agree, however, that a technique which is suitable for a race track, on which all the drivers are highly skilled and travelling in the same direction in cars which have been prepared with extreme care, is not suitable for driving on crowded public highways.

Nevertheless, a similar technique applies. Each bend and corner should be assessed, and the correct line, or course, selected as you approach it.

The right course is in the *correct* lane, and not the shortest distance.

At the approach to a right-hand bend keep well into the nearside.

Check the mirror, brake while the car is travelling in a straight line, change into the correct gear and, when you see the end of the bend, take the straightest safe line out without crossing the centre white line.

This will bring you out of the bend on the correct side of the road and able to remain there.

Braking should be completed before you commence to turn the steering wheel and acceleration applied either gently or firmly, according to conditions, as you commence the turn.

Negotiation of a left-hand bend at which visibility is limited is likely to be more dangerous than a similar right-hand bend. The Highway Code says, 'Keep well to the left' and also tells drivers to adjust speed so that they can pull up well within the distance they can see to be clear.

To the question 'What is the correct way to take the bend at . . .' one can only answer 'At what time of the day or night? What are the traffic conditions, the vehicle, and who is the driver?'

By using the road correctly, a skilful driver will take a bend smoothly, without discomfort to his passengers, with complete safety and at a speed which would be menacing if attempted by an inexperienced or unskilled driver.

Keep to your own side of the road, and avoid crossing the centre white line. Should you be involved in a collision as a result of disregarding this rule it is doubtful whether you could offer an excuse acceptable to a court of law.

In winding lanes, it should never be assumed that the road ahead, out of sight around the bend, is clear of hazards.

One rule which should be obeyed at all times and under all circumstances is in paragraph 34 of the Highway Code:

'Never drive so fast that you cannot stop well within the distance you can see to be clear. Go much more slowly if the road is wet or icy, or if there is fog.'

If you are following a large van or lorry round a right-hand bend, by keeping a good distance between your vehicle and the one in front and positioning so that you can see past its off-side, you will get a view of the road ahead just before reaching the apex of the bend.

Again, for a left-hand bend, leave a good gap, keep well to the left and get your view of the road past the near-side of the van.

Always check for the parked car or other obstruction which might cause the driver ahead of you to change course.

And always make allowance for a carelessly parked or broken-down vehicle which might be just out of sight around a blind bend.

Never trust another driver, or cycle rider, to do the right thing.

To keep out of trouble you need a healthy imagination, and to put your trust in one thing only—your own skill and driving ability.

X

'COMMENTARY' DRIVING

'COMMENTARY' driving forms an important part of the training programme in a Police driving school.

Some people say it is a distraction; that it interferes with concentration.

Surely the reverse is true, for how is it possible to give an intelligent commentary while thinking of business or any other problems?

A worth-while fluent and articulate commentary demands practice, but this is available whenever you drive your car.

By worth-while commentary is meant one which reveals good road observation, anticipation and an explanation of the action to be taken to deal with any possible hazard.

At first you may find that to describe what you see and your plan of procedure gives you a feeling of self-consciousness.

This will pass off, and, even when driving in fairly heavy traffic, your concentration and observation of the road will give you fluency.

When you are on the open road, or a motorway, long distance observation will be brought into use, and the commentary taken further ahead.

In this way, you will be able to assess each hazard, or possible manoeuvre with a view to selection of course, speed and correct gear, and have time to talk about it.

At the outset, you might say, for example: 'Two children ahead on bicycles'. Such a remark would not be very helpful, but if you continued, 'So I am checking my mirror, signalling to the following driver that I am selecting a course which will allow plenty of clearance should they swerve, and giving a light tap on the horn, to warn the children of my presence', it would be apparent you had seen possible danger and were taking appropriate action.

Many who have experienced a demonstration drive as passengers in police cars have remarked on the reassurance that a commentary imparts.

In the Advanced Driving Test, a commentary informs the experienced Examiner about a candidate's attitude towards driving.

The following is part of a recorded commentary from one of the London area test routes:

'We are now on a dual carriageway, speed limit 40, heavy lorry ahead, travelling below the limit. I check my mirror: a car overtaking me at fairly high speed, keep in and let him pass. Check mirror again, nothing behind, look up near-side and off-side of lorry, road clear, pull out to overtake, no need to signal, road still clear behind. Hump-back bridge ahead, also school sign, time 3.50 p.m., keep special look-out for children.

'There is the school road, clear. Derestriction sign, traffic very light, build up speed progressively, learner driver and milk float ahead, both travelling slowly, my speed sixty-five, check mirror, car a long way behind, signal, pull out to overtake both vehicles, then pull back to near-side.

'Approaching roundabout, select course, check mirror, brake, change into third gear, signal left trafficator that I am leaving the roundabout in that direction*. Road dry, accelerate and change up to top again.

'Thirty sign ahead, so decelerate and enter controlled zone at correct speed, houses and shops on both sides of road. Look underneath parked vehicles for feet, allow a door's width when overtaking them.

* See Chapter XVII 'Roundabout Driving'.

'Cross roads ahead, check mirror, brake, into third gear, a look to both sides, accelerate and clear the hazard.

'Forty sign in view, build my speed up to this, left-hand bend, mirror, nothing behind, keeping out towards centre of road for maximum visibility, straight across the apex, leaving the bend on the correct side of the road.

'Minor road junction on left, by looking through gap in hedge I see it is clear, no need to reduce speed, long clear view ahead, wide grass verges on both sides, check instruments, everything working correctly.

'Road narrows sign, and hump-back bridge, check mirror, reduce speed, into third gear, keep well in to left, stationary lorry on other side of bridge, puff of exhaust gas, he is going to move off, let him go, not safe to overtake—double bend ahead.'

This commentary told the Examiner a great deal about the candidate's ability to drive competently and decisively.

Indecision is a dangerous fault. It manifests itself in a driver's inability to judge distance and speed.

This results in inconsistencies, such as failing to take advantage of a gap in the traffic at a road junction where there is a wide margin of safety, while at the next junction taking an unnecessary risk by crossing in front of traffic with inches to spare.

Over-cautious drivers also create a great many traffic hold-ups, but indecisive, inconsistent ones create actual danger.

Generally speaking, the only cure for these faults is good instruction. All driving faults are relative, but indecision plus incorrect gear selection, positioning or braking make a lethal mixture.

XI

DRIVING IN FOG

IF you ask any experienced driver which hazard he or she disliked most, without hesitation, the answer would be 'Fog'.

The best possible advice for driving in fog can be contained in a few words: DON'T, if you can possibly avoid it.

Motorways, which ought to be the safest roads in the country, are best avoided, as too many drivers fail to observe the elementary rule of driving within a safe vision range.

All too frequently this results in unnecessary multiple crashes, in which the innocent as well as the guilty suffer.

The paramount thing to remember is that you should be seen by other road users.

In daylight fog drive with all the lamps on, including headlamps. During night fog in most instances, however, they will make matters worse.

A pair of fog lamps, one directed at the kerb and the other adjusted to suit both the conditions and you, the driver, can be very helpful. From 1st January 1970 it will not be lawful to use a *single* fog lamp on a car unless your headlamps are on as well.

If you travel regularly by the same route, memorise landmarks, such as brightly illuminated signs or shops and so forth. Make a mental note of telephone kiosks and garages.

In fog conditions you should then know where you are with a reasonable degree of certainty at any given time. Distances are deceiving, and always appear to be greater in fog.

'Cats' eyes' in the centre of the road can be a guide, but never drive astride them in case you meet an approaching driver following the same technique.

Parked vehicles without lights are frequently encountered, often due to batteries going flat through prolonged driving at speeds too low to provide sufficient charge.

Drive at a speed which you feel is consistent with prevailing conditions and safety. Let other drivers overtake you if they wish—they are sometimes useful to follow.

Do not let them influence your own judgment, however. They might be the occupants of the crashed cars you pass at a later stage of your journey.

In low-lying fog, bus and lorry drivers can often drive faster and more safely than car drivers because of their higher seating position. If they happen to be going in your direction, be content to follow.

Having no windscreens or bonnets to obstruct their view, too, cyclists and motor-cyclists can travel faster than most car drivers. But do not suddenly switch your headlamps on, or you will throw the rider's shadow on the fog ahead and make things difficult for him.

If you are carrying a passenger, get him to keep you informed as to your distance from the kerb. If the fog is very thick you may persuade him to walk in front. Should a torch be available, get him to carry it; if not, a newspaper, handkerchief or light-coloured scarf can be helpful.

Always keep the back door windows a bit open to prevent the rear window misting up.

The most dangerous manoeuvre is turning to the right, particularly at cross-roads, when you could have traffic approaching from the front and both sides.

Lower your window as you approach the junction, give an early signal with your trafficators, flash your headlamps, sound the horn and wait for an answering toot, a bicycle bell—even a shout from a pedestrian—before commencing the turn.

Check the fluid level for the windscreen washers before starting off, and keep the windscreen clean inside and out. As you will be driving in the lower gears keep an eye on the fuel gauge; there is no worse time to run out of petrol.

A breakdown on the road during thick fog can be suicidal if you attempt repairs. If you have to abandon the car, park it off the highway.

The following instructions are issued by the MoT for the guidance of motorists using the motorway when fog is present.

Warning Signals on
MOTORWAYS

For some time to come. many motorways will have flashing amber light signals at their entrances and at one-mile intervals. The lights warn of danger ahead; for example, an accident, fog, or risk of skidding. When the lights are flashing, keep your speed under 30 m.p.h. When you see the danger, slow down still further, to a crawl if need be. Do not exceed 30 m.p.h. until you are sure it is safe.

New warning signals being put on rural motorways will usually be at two-mile intervals on the central reserve. They have amber lights, and a panel in the middle. When there is a danger ahead the amber lights flash and the panel shows the advised maximum speed at which you should travel or a 'wicket' sign showing which lane ahead is blocked. Take extra care when the lights are flashing.

The new warning signals on urban motorways will be above the road at least every 1,000 yards. Each lane has its signal above the lane. The signals have amber lights and panels which show an advised maximum speed or arrows pointing to the lane you should use. The signals also have red lights. When the red lights are flashing above your lane, you must stop at the signal.

Nearside to nearside.
Vision restricted

Off-side to off-side. Wide unrestricted
view of traffic coming from left

Can My Safet

1	2	3
Mentally select the correct course	Check the Mirror(s) and blind spot	Give a clear Signal and take up course

Given Away

4
Brake whilst the car is travelling on a straight course

5
Engage the correct Gear

6
Acceleration

If the car is likely to skid, it will be in the arc between point one and two, therefore, if the road is dry and in good condition, acceleration may be applied from point one. If it is wet, greasy, loose, icy or liable to encourage skid, firm acceleration from point two when the car is once more travelling on a straight course. Gentle acceleration from point one to point two.

Red triangle denotes danger just out of sight round the bend

XII

DRIVING ON SNOW AND ICE

W HO knows what winter will bring? We may be sweltering in a heat wave or enduring blizzards and heavy frost. The important thing, as far as *you*, the driver, are concerned, is to be ready for anything—and that means winter at its worst.

If you use busy main roads you shouldn't have too much to worry about, because good driving, good tyres and common-sense will no doubt get you through.

But remember that, when driving on ice or hard-packed snow, your braking distances can go up by as much as ten times. Where you normally require, say, forty-five feet to pull up in, you may now need four hundred and fifty feet.

The biggest danger is, of course, skidding. Your first skid, when the rear of the car wants to change places with the front, can be a frightening business.

Depending on your speed at the time, the car may even turn several complete circles or stop forcibly after hitting another vehicle.

Skids must be avoided at all costs, and the primary requirement is to use your road observation to anticipate treacherous road conditions.

Turning a bend or surmounting a dip in the road may bring you on to a section which has caught the frost by reason of its north or east aspect.

Shaded patches on a thawing snow-bound road are particularly dangerous, and braking should be avoided when driving over them.

If your motoring takes you off the main roads, it will be worth-while to invest in a set of chains and carry them in the boot when snow threatens. But practice fitting them in the comfort of your garage, and not on the road during a snow storm, with frozen fingers.

Chains are not difficult to fit if you follow the manufacturer's instructions. Having fitted them, spin the wheels to make sure that they will not touch any part of the body or wings.

Remember that snow chains are only efficient when the road surface is completely snow-covered. Remove them immediately the snow disappears, or they will quickly wear out.

A skid occurs when a force which is stronger than the grip of the tyres on the road acts on the car in a direction other than that in which it is travelling.

Whilst road conditions may encourage skidding, it rests with the driver as to whether it actually comes about, and to what extent.

Late, fierce braking; harsh steering movements; unduly fierce acceleration which results in wheel spin; driving too fast having regard to road conditions, or a combination of these faults are the main causes.

The two most likely types of skid with which you will have to deal are:—

REAR WHEEL SKID: When the car attempts to turn broadside, it will turn right round if you fail to take immediate action.

FOUR WHEEL SKID: Which produces a feeling of increased speed instead of the reverse when the brakes are applied, and usually occurs because the wheels are locked as a result of too high pedal pressure for tyre grip on the road.

Front wheel skids do sometimes occur on bends or corners, usually as a result of excessive speed or brakes which, through faulty adjustment, cause the car to slew over to one side, and this may be encouraged through the fitting of brake pressure limiting valves on the rear, nowadays a growing practice.

Always drive so as to reduce the possibility of skidding to a minimum. The best way to do this is to keep speed down and use the accelerator and brakes delicately. Do not attempt to keep to a tight time schedule when the roads are covered with ice, snow or frost. Remember that under these conditions braking distances can go up by as much as ten times.

If you follow this advice, you will be able to correct any skid which does occur by removing your foot from the accelerator and steering into it; that is, if the rear of the car breaks off to the left, turn the steering wheel to the left enough to correct the skid, but not enough to induce a skid in the opposite direction.

When the car is again under control, apply acceleration *very* gently and smoothly. Keep your foot off the brake pedal and remain in a lower gear until you feel it safe to proceed normally. At all costs avoid the temptation to increase speed when you are making reasonably safe progress. If you have to use your brake at any time, do so very lightly to prevent locking the wheels.

A good tip is to apply the brake pedal with a gentle action, on and off repeatedly, so that retardation is given without reaching the point of locking.

When starting off on snow or ice, either engage the HIGHEST gear the engine will take (your car may pull steadily in third or top gear), or use first gear with engine idling.

You should always, even on the best of roads, keep a safe distance from the car in front. This means your overall braking and thinking distance under existing conditions:

Do your best to avoid a rear-end collision by giving **the driver following you** maximum room in which to pull up in emergency, watching him closely in your rear mirror.

Hill climbing can be extremely difficult, despite transferring as much weight as possible (including passengers) to the rear of the car, if it has drive to the back wheels.

The action to take will depend on traffic conditions; the first consideration is safety, so, if there is traffic following, turn the steering wheel so that, if the car starts to slide, it will travel only as far as the kerb.

43

Brushwood, grit, an old sack—even the car mats—may enable you to re-start, and, if so, avoid the temptation to change gear or increase speed until you have completed the climb.

To save having to walk back down the hill to retrieve the mat or sack, attach it to the rear bumper (or door handle) by a length of cord or stout string and pull it along with you when you get going.

Link mats are particularly good for helping to get a start in snow. It is also a wise precaution for country dwellers to carry a shovel in the boot.

If you drive in a district subject to heavy snowfalls, keep the petrol tank full in order to be able to keep the engine running for warmth should you be stranded in a drift. BUT, be certain the exhaust fumes cannot percolate into the car from a leaky silencer.

If the road behind is clear, manoeuvre the car slowly back down the hill and try again, keeping it running at a steady speed all the way up, on a straight course.

Going *down hill* under treacherous conditions is dangerous if you fail to keep the car under a controllable speed from the top of the decline.

Keep well to the nearside, engage an intermediate (but not lowest) gear and press the brake pedal gently, on and off, as already recommended. It may be best to declutch if the engine is of very high compression ratio type.

When snow is falling, keep the wipers and defroster working and, if the temperature is below freezing point, do not use your windscreen washers or apply moisture unless you have anti-freeze. Certain efficient de-icing fluids are available.

If you park in a snowstorm, cover the windscreen with news- or brown-paper, or you might keep a piece of hessian in the boot for this purpose; you can hold it in position by inserting it between the front of the door and the windscreen pillar.

When the temperature is around freezing point there is another danger to be considered—slush or snow thrown up under the front wings. This, when frozen, can form into a groove which will restrict the lock of the front wheels. If you feel any such restriction, remove its cause *immediately*.

Also don't forget to remove as much snow as possible before leaving the car overnight, otherwise frost may 'anchor' the the wheels to the ground.

If water or slush gets into the brake drums or on handbrake mechanism, they too may freeze solid, particularly if the brake is left on. Better leave bottom gear engaged instead.

Another point is the door lock—you may have to heat the key to insert it.

Misted-up insides of the screen, rear and side windows are a menace to safe driving. Always keep them as clear as possible by using anti-mist panels or the special fluids compounded for the purpose.

At any time of the year, but naturally more so in winter, water on the roads is a common hazard. It brings with it two main dangers, of which the obvious one is greasy surface, especially if light rain follows a long dry spell.

The other is 'aquaplaning', a phenomenon which the tyre experts have discovered is likely to occur on a very wet road. A cushion of water forms between tyre tread and road surface if the tread is unable to disperse the wedge of water which forms in front of the tyre.

A modern tyre's tread, in good condition, is more capable of dealing with this wedge of water, but a worn or bald tread rides, or aquaplanes, on the water and loses contact with the road at fairly high speeds. A front wheel under these conditions may even cease to revolve and lose its capability of steering the car.

There are two ways of preventing aquaplaning: one is to keep watch on the condition of your tyre treads, the other is to keep speed below the critical range when roads are awash—depending on the tyre's condition, aquaplaning can set in at any speed above 50 m.p.h. Even a new tyre can aquaplane if the water is deep enough. A remedy is to jab the brake pedal.

To quote the experts whose main concern is to produce 'safe' tyres: 'When aquaplaning starts, you are within seconds of the accident'. It is vitally necessary to equate speeds with road and weather conditions and to use imagination and anticipation to the full where braking distances are concerned.

A sudden cloudburst can reduce visibility to almost nil and it becomes desirable to switch the lights on. If you have to leave your car standing out in heavy rain so that the windscreen and rear window are semi-opaque, it is handy to have a squeegee, like a screenwiper blade. The same goes, of course, for snowfalls, while an ice scraper, or one of the de-icing fluids, is well nigh indispensable when frost is about. A special demisting cloth is useful for the inside of the screen and windows.

XIII

FLOOD

After a heavy rain-storm, or what is sometimes referred to as a cloud burst, many roads are subject to flooding; those who live in such areas are no doubt well equipped to deal with this particular hazard and take it in their stride.

If you meet it for the first time, however, there are certain precautions to be taken.

The first is to determine the depth of water at the deepest point. You may be able to do this by watching the attempt of another driver; on the other hand, it may occur at a time when there is no other traffic on that particular road; if this is the case, it may be necessary to remove your shoes and socks and find out for yourself.

Should you decide that it is safe to proceed, cover the front of the radiator grille with some thick paper or a car rug to prevent a sudden surge of water swamping the engine.

Disconnect the fan if it is placed low down or liable to come into contact with the water, otherwise it will smother the engine with a fine spray. (This refers to belt driven fans.)

Engage first gear, enter the water very slowly, keep the engine running fairly fast in order to prevent water entering the exhaust pipe, and control the speed of the car by slipping the clutch.

Should you be unable to get a tow, remove the plugs to eliminate compression, disconnect the coil, and drive out in low gear on the starter, or 'wind' the car out with the starting handle (if one is fitted).

Driving out on the starter should not be attempted under any circumstances without removing the plugs, if the exhaust pipe is full of water, otherwise the engine may back-fire through the carburettor, leaving you to deal with both fire and flood.

When you emerge from the water, check the brakes; they will probably be useless until you dry them out. To do this, drive at a slow speed keeping light pressure on the footbrake until they grip once more. Test them several times until you are completely satisfied with their efficiency before attempting to drive at normal speeds.

If you know that you may encounter flooded roads, carry a waterproof sheet to cover the radiator grille, and a piece of rubber tubing which can be fitted over the exhaust tail pipe with the open end supported well above the flood level to prevent water entering.

XIV

SIGNALS: VISIBLE

BEWARE of dogmatists in connection with signals to be given when driving a car.

The advanced driver's rule should be 'give **necessary** signals, clearly, correctly and in good time'.

Necessary signals are those which assist other road users and protect you from other road users' carelessness.

The correct signals are set out in the Highway Code. Unorthodox signals should be avoided—they are misleading and would not be accepted in a court of law.

The fact that a driver considers his own particular version of a signal superior to those which are authorised would not absolve him from blame, if his version were misunderstood and resulted in an accident.

Many drivers continue to use the 'overtake me' (wave on) signal, which is not now in the Highway Code. Signal your own intentions, but let the other driver decide his own actions, and don't drive blindly into danger just because the driver in front waves you on.

If you are following a really good driver you will be able to anticipate his moves by the positioning of his car on the road.

This, together with his correct use of traffic indicators and brake lights, will give you ample warning of deviations.

Traffic indicators and brake lights, like all mechanical appliances, are not infallible, so that a close watch should be kept on their efficiency.

An arm signal is sometimes necessary—for example, to indicate to a Police Officer controlling traffic that you intend to proceed straight ahead.

Also, if you are followed by one of those menaces who drives a few feet away from your rear bumper at forty m.p.h., and you intend to slow down or stop, it will be necessary to give the arm 'slow down or stop' signal (as per the Highway Code) both for his benefit and even for that of witnesses. His bonnet might obscure his view of your braking lights!

When you are being followed too closely for safety or comfort, at the first opportunity let the person concerned overtake you. It is annoying to have to give way to crass stupidity, but it's safer, quicker and altogether better than a rear-end collision.

Never trust a signal given by a traffic indicator, even if you see it switched on, until it is confirmed by the position of the car. **Always** remember to cancel your own immediately it is no longer necessary.

As was said at the commencement, 'beware the dogmatist'; if a signal will assist other road users or protect yourself, **GIVE IT.**

During the hours of darkness, and particularly when sounding the horn in built-up areas is prohibited,* headlamps can be used to warn other users of your presence.

They should not be used for conveying a message such as 'I am coming through', or 'you can come through'; misunderstanding has created many dangerous situations.

SIGNALS: AUDIBLE

To many road users the sound of a motor horn is tantamount to a challenge—or an insult.

Press reports and personal experience have shown that some react quite violently, verbally and even physically, despite the fact that the Construction and Use Regulations require a motor vehicle to be 'fitted with an instrument capable of giving audible and sufficient warning of its approach or position'.

* Between 11.30 pm and 7 am.

Some dogmatists say 'Good drivers NEVER use the horn', to which the commonsense answer must be 'Good drivers use the horn *intelligently*'.

The horn is 'the voice of the car'; indiscriminate or aggressive use should be avoided.

A slight 'excuse me' tap warns the pedestrian about to step into the road, or the cyclist weaving about, that he may endanger himself and you.

A louder and longer note when overtaking at high speed, or overtaking vehicles with noisy engines, is desirable in the interests of safety.

The horn should also be used during the hours of daylight in conditions that call for audible warning, or in the presence of children playing in the street. But not as a substitute for observation, anticipation or care!

And always remember that it is an offence to sound the horn whenever the car is stationary, at any hour.

XV

REVERSING AND PARKING

ASK the average driver to start his car on a hill, or move it forward 50 yards, and he will in most cases do so smoothly and competently.

But ask him to carry out the same manoeuvre in reverse and note the difference.

In many cases the engine will be over-revved; there will be a judder through the transmission, and the car will reverse in a series of small jerky movements.

Needless to say, this is harmful to the car and disturbing to the passengers. The main reason will be lack of practice.

It is doubtful whether a driver who travels, say, 12,000 miles a year, covers in that distance more than a couple of miles in reverse.

For his lack of skill a driver usually blames roughness of the clutch, but this particular driving fault usually results from trying to control the speed of the car by varying foot pressure on the clutch pedal.

It is certainly necessary to do this when reversing a mere few inches, or when parking in a confined space.

When it is necessary to reverse for several yards, however, the clutch should be fully engaged, and the speed of the car controlled by means of the accelerator.

In addition many drivers weave about when reversing; seemingly they are incapable of keeping the steering wheel in one position and letting the car run back on a straight course.

The only answer to these reversing difficulties is practice, which should be done on a quiet road or a large (and empty) car park. The only equipment needed is two garden canes and two tins filled with soil or sand.

The canes should be wrapped round with any old material so that the car can touch them without scratching its bodywork.

Having found a suitable site for practice, insert the canes into the tins and set them up so to allow about four inches clearance on each side of the car.

Now reverse through them from a distance of about 20 yards, and when able to carry this out smoothly in one move, gradually reduce the distance apart of the canes.

Eventually a bare inch or so clearance on either side will be found sufficient, but make allowance for door handles, mirrors, bumpers or other protuberances.

Next, increase the width of the canes and reverse through them from an angle of about 45° right and left.

Follow this by setting up a single cane and see how close the car can be reversed to it without knocking it over, or even touching it.

When a driver is able to carry out all these manoeuvres smoothly and competently his reversing troubles should be over.

For practising 'reverse parking' set the canes a car's width from the kerb and one-and-a-half car lengths apart, to represent parking between two stationary cars.

First drive forward until the rear bumper is level with the foremost cane, leaving about two feet to the side of it.

Commence to reverse slowly, turning the steering wheel to full left lock all the while.

When the cane is sighted at about the middle of the front passenger window (this will vary according to the particular car) straighten the front wheels and continue reversing until sure that the front bumper will miss the cane.

Now turn the steering wheel to full right lock and continue slowly back until the car is parked neatly, close to the kerb.

Make one move forward to centralise the car and to allow the drivers of the adjacent cars reasonable room to pull out cleanly.

Accuracy is much more important than speed, so take it calmly and practise until the whole operation is done in one continuous movement.

When using a car park always try to leave enough room for other drivers to open their doors without fouling your car, and vice versa.

An essential safety rule, before reversing in public streets, is to make sure there are no children playing at the rear, or a parked bicycle—or even a snoozing cat—and beware broken glass which could damage the tyres.

Take every precaution to ensure that the manoeuvre is safe before it is attempted.

XVI

NIGHT DRIVING

DESPITE efforts to shorten traffic queues during the tourist season, travelling conditions by day become steadily worse.

Many drivers now travel by night from choice, but the time is rapidly approaching when more will use the night hours from necessity.

Now, night driving can be very enjoyable, especially being able to pass through towns and cities at good average speeds instead of crawling in traffic queues.

While we hear much about the dangers of mixing driving with drink or drugs, too little is said about the effects of fatigue, which is a major enemy of driving safety.

Never start out on a long night journey without having had sufficient rest or sleep beforehand. The dangers of an attack of drowsiness, or actually falling asleep over the wheel, are obvious, but too seldom realised.

It is most unwise to resort to 'pep pills', which react on human beings in many different ways, but all of them adversely as far as driving is concerned.

Before starting a night journey, carefully check the working of all the electrical equipment, lights (including braking and tail lights), dipping switch, traffic indicators and windscreen wipers and washer.

If carrying a heavy load in the boot, this may make the head-lamp beams point upwards too much, and dazzle others even when dipped. Therefore, test this and have an adjustment made if necessary. Go to a garage or service station with proper beam-setting equipment—don't do it yourself.

Make sure that all tyres, including the spare, are inflated to the correct pressures for a loaded car, as recommended by the manufacturers.

Place the tools where you can get at them without having to unload all your luggage. Carry a set of spare bulbs, fuses and a torch, and check regularly that all your lights are working properly. Take a critical look, too, at the fanbelt's condition.

Do keep the car well ventilated; to drive with the heater on and all the windows closed encourages drowsiness.

If your passengers will not be inconvenienced, open such of the windows as will ventilate the car without inducing a fierce draught. (Some modern cars, of course, do have efficient means of ventilation without this.)

If, however, you **are** overcome by drowsiness, **stop the car,** take a brisk walk, have some refreshment, or 'sleep it off'—the time lost is unimportant when compared with the risk of pressing on regardless. On a motorway, however, lower your window and stop on a service area when you reach one, or turn off at an exit.

Driving by night demands a great deal of patience, restraint and tolerance. The man in front who is driving slowly on the crown of the road, or the approaching driver who fails to dip his headlamps, might be inexperienced, elderly or nervous.

Any attempt to retaliate by driving too close, or impatiently switching headlamps on to full beam, could produce disastrous results.

When driving in built-up areas, always be alert for pedestrians in dark clothing, the cyclist without a rear light or a vehicle parked without lights. It is now advised to drive on dipped or dimmed headlights in built-up areas during the official hours of darkness.

56

Switch on your sidelamps as daylight fades, without waiting for the official lighting-up time.

On roads outside lit areas, you must use headlamps—full beam or dipped—during the hours of darkness.

At night-time on a straight road the headlamps of an approaching vehicle can cause dazzle from a long way off. If its driver fails to dip, avoid looking directly into the glare, but focus your vision on the nearside of the road, reduce speed and concentrate on any hazards which were in view before you were dazzled.

During the hours of darkness, it is more difficult to judge the distance of approaching or following vehicles, or vehicles from the right or left when you come to a main road.

Much extra care is required when driving in heavy rain at night. Braking distances increase, road surfaces become more uncertain and difficult to assess, and vision is reduced all round. This is the time when pedestrians and cyclists are apt to be more concerned about keeping the rain off their faces than a ton of fast-moving metal off their backs.

While the presence of approaching headlamps indicates that overtaking is 'out', their absence should never cause one to assume that the road ahead is clear, or that one single approaching light signifies the presence of only a bicycle or motor cycle.

When following another vehicle, try to keep it beyond the end of your dipped headlamp beam, and not in it. Never switch the headlamps on to full beam when overtaking in the face of oncoming traffic.

Headlamps should be dipped early, and particularly before commencing to negotiate a left-hand bend in order to prevent the full beam swinging across the windscreen of any approaching vehicle.

This precaution is not so important for right-hand bends, because the light beams are directed to the left or nearside, away from oncoming traffic.

Always drive within the range of your headlamps, so that a stop could be made inside the distance seen to be clear.

In the event of a breakdown or other forced stop, get the car off the carriageway if humanly possible. Sometimes the starter motor will help by providing sufficient power if bottom gear is engaged.

The wise driver who travels by night will carry an authorised means of warning such as 'red triangle', or have fitted a device for operating all his direction indicators simultaneously when he is stationary.

XVII

ROUNDABOUTS

THE question 'which is the correct way to negotiate a roundabout?' is like the question 'How long is a piece of string?' and must evoke the reply—'which roundabout, how many converging roads, at what time of the day or night, and is traffic controlled by 'give way' signs or traffic lights?'

If it can be seen that a roundabout is clear of traffic, the correct through course is the straightest possible line. Close to the nearside kerb on entering, close to the centre island and close to the nearside kerb on leaving – this helps to keep the car stable and reduces the risk of skidding. Whether you apply firm acceleration from approximately the apex of the centre island or when you leave the roundabout and your car is travelling in a straight line, will depend on road and weather conditions.

If the approach road to the roundabout carries two lanes of traffic and you wish to leave by the first exit on the left ('9 o'clock'), take up the nearside lane and signal your intention with the left traffic indicator before you enter the roundabout.

If you intend to continue straight through the roundabout, signal with the left trafficator on reaching the 9 o'clock position on the centre island.

Should you wish to leave the roundabout at the 3 o'clock position, use the system of control before taking up the offside lane, and on reaching the 12 o'clock position, signal your intention to leave the roundabout with the left traffic indicator.

Many elongated traffic islands, however, are incorrectly termed roundabouts. Some carry three, even four, lanes of traffic. In such cases if a *right* indicator signal could be of assistance to other road users **it should be given.**

A single broken white line marks the point of entry to most roundabouts. Rule 81 of the Highway Code says: 'Give way to traffic coming from your immediate right unless road markings indicate otherwise, but keep moving if the way is clear.'

In 'exceptional cases', denoted by special markings at the roundabout concerned, traffic on the roundabouts will be required to give way to traffic entering it. Police or traffic light control may also be used where difficulties arise owing to the domination of one stream of traffic by another.

At peak traffic times, however, severe difficulties can be experienced by drivers wishing to enter from a minor road.

Frequently they are faced with a choice of waiting an excessively long time, and holding up a queue of irate, horn-tooting following drivers, or disobeying the 'give way' sign with all the risks that such action entails. Nevertheless, obey them.

Unfortunately, some drivers when in a roundabout will accelerate to close the gap and prevent traffic from filtering into the traffic stream.

These types have been described by a Member of Parliament as 'men who shed a thousand years of civilisation the moment they enter a car', and by an Irish Motoring Correspondent as 'drivers with the car in gear and the mind in neutral'.

If it were possible to train all vehicular road users to filter alternately at roundabouts, there would be no need for signs or regulations—this, like most problems, could be solved with a little give and take.

XVIII

REACTION TIMES

THE fallacious remark 'I stopped dead' has been heard many times at the scene of an accident during the past, and will undoubtedly be heard many more times in the future.

Every road user, whether on foot or on wheels, has a time-lag or thinking distance, between seeing a danger and taking action to deal with it.

Furthermore, the vehicle which will 'stop dead' has not yet been designed and is never likely to be.

Our time-lag varies according to our physical and mental condition, and is adversely affected by fatigue, drugs, alcohol, worry, emotional disturbance or excitement, plus other influences.

If a driver takes only half a second to appreciate danger and to move his foot from the accelerator to the brake (and this is quicker than average) at 60 miles per hour, his car will travel 44 feet **before braking starts to take effect.**

In many instances this distance can be reduced by 'covering' the footbrake pedal with one's foot instead of keeping it hovering over a trailing throttle.

Sudden fierce braking, or last-minute panic action, is almost invariably the result of lack of concentration, observation and/or anticipation.

To some drivers a crash stop is an everyday occurrence; others may drive for years without applying their brakes suddenly and fiercely, because they are fully conscious of the facts of life as applied to 'time-lags'.

While one can see nothing wrong with speed at the right time and place, in the hands of a responsible, concentrated driver, it is imperative to drive at a slower speed than is usual when our time-lag has increased as a result of extraneous circumstances, physical or mental.

When driving at night the time-lag of recovering from the effects of dazzle has also to be considered. This can be anything between two and seven seconds.

In terms of 60 m.p.h. this means that the car travels anything from 176 to 616 feet with a temporarily blinded driver at the wheel.

At many Road Safety Exhibitions throughout the country, machines are made freely available to test braking reaction, recovery from glare and condition of eyesight. On the basis 'that to know a danger is to guard against it', a trial is well worth the time taken.

XIX

TRAFFIC DRIVING

IF your route will take you through unfamiliar towns, where one-way traffic systems probably abound, study a street map beforehand.

It may be, if you look sufficiently far ahead, that you could even by-pass some town centres altogether. If this is not possible, try to sense the general direction you will have to bear at forks or cross roads and the names of places next along your route.

Clear instructions written on a card affixed to the dash or some other convenient place can be most helpful; if you are carrying a passenger, ask him or her to navigate.

If the road carries three lanes of traffic in each direction, the nearside is for slow moving traffic and vehicles making repeated stops, such as buses, also vehicles turning to the left; the centre lane is for traffic going straight ahead and the offside one for traffic turning right, generally speaking.

If driving on the nearside, intending to go straight on in a two-lane road, keep a sharp look out for filter arrows at the traffic lights, otherwise you may be obliged to turn left in order to avoid an embarrassing situation.

Should you get into the wrong lane by accident, and if you cannot 'fall out' without inconveniencing other traffic, keep going and later make a diversion in order to get back to your proper route.

Ill-mannered drivers will cut across another lane in order to rectify their error; don't imitate them, but watch them in case they might foul you in the process.

Always keep a safe distance from the vehicle ahead. Remember that at thirty miles an hour, with a half-second reaction delay, you will travel 22 feet while just moving your foot from the throttle to the brake—and you still have to stop the car. Correct distance is overall braking and thinking distance.

Check your rear mirror(s) frequently, *always* before changing course or altering speed, and particularly before turning to the left, as a cyclist or motor cyclist may be attempting to overtake you on the nearside.

When stopping on an up-gradient, make allowance for the vehicle in front running back when starting, and leave enough room to manoeuvre if it is unable to get going forward.

Remember that when you are slowing down or stopping for a pedestrian to use a zebra crossing, an arm signal should be used. Not only is this a positive warning to following drivers but it helps the pedestrian—he cannot see your brake lights.'

Should you stop behind a 'learner' driver, leave a margin for his getting into reverse by mistake.

If the roads are wet, or liable to encourage skidding, give a reasonably wide berth to cyclists, motor cyclists, scooterists and riders of mopeds.

It is imperative to remember that a green traffic light means only that it *should* be safe to proceed, with caution. The fact that thousands of drivers are summoned every year for disregarding the red proves that it is a widespread practice.

When you are approaching traffic lights which are showing green in your favour, progressively reduce speed so that you can stop if another driver crosses from your right or left against the red.

Change into a lower gear and, when you reach a point where you can see that vehicles on your right and left are stationary and no attempt is being made to contravene the lights, you should accelerate and clear the hazard briskly.

Conversely, if you have to stop at the red, don't let your attention wander. Be ready to move off when the green light appears and it is safe to do so. The capacity of traffic lights is greatly reduced by inattentive and incompetent drivers.

You should engage gear when the amber light appears; this should give you time to start off efficiently, thereby assisting traffic flow.

If you are turning right at a road junction and you meet an approaching driver who also wishes to turn right, as a general rule pass offside to offside and round the back of the approaching car, which will give you an unrestricted view of traffic coming from your left.

At some crossings, however, the layout of the roads may render this impossible. In such cases let the other driver clear the crossing before you proceed. If the approaching driver signifies his intention to 'give way' accept and acknowledge his courtesy, but don't play 'after you' unnecessarily.

Driving in heavy traffic demands endless patience and tolerance, Nothing is gained by a display of temper or aggressive horn blowing, even though there is no doubt that a great deal of congestion is caused by inattentive driving.

'Window shopping', or lack of concentration which causes delay at traffic lights, or driving astride lane markings with a view to changing into the shortest or fastest moving lane, are examples of selfish, irresponsible driving which, multiplied many times, reduces road capacity and creates ill-temper among other drivers.

It cannot be emphasised too strongly that truly advanced driving means proceeding with due regard to other traffic and of course to road and weather conditions.

Every driver has his or her 'off day', when it appears that there are more 'fools' than usual on the road.

Pedestrians seem determined to walk in front of the car, cyclists to change course suddenly and without warning, other drivers force you to crash stop or take sudden evasive action.

When one of these periods occurs, it is advisable to ask oneself 'Is it them or me?'

Self-examination might reveal that the fault lies with you, that your mind is preoccupied with other things beside driving your car.

We drive as we feel; a worried, angry or sick driver can be a dangerous one.

A driver suffering from fatigue can be as menacing as one suffering from the effects of too much alcohol, if he fails to recognise his condition and remedy himself mentally.

An eminent pathologist has stated that the first rule for drivers should be 'know thyself and drive accordingly'.

The basic fundamentals of 'right part of the road', with the correct gear engaged and travelling at a speed which is consistent with safety and prevailing conditions, must be observed at *all times*.

Beyond this it is not possible to state categorically how a given manoeuvre should be carried out.

For example, on a particular stretch of road, today, you might overtake another vehicle, whereas tomorrow, on the same stretch of road, something about the behaviour of the driver in front might cause you to 'hold back'.

Reading the road also includes the people using it; if you notice another driver behaving erratically, there is no excuse for becoming involved with him. Keep the greatest possible distance between your car and his.

If you are obliged to pull alongside him at traffic lights, watch him carefully when the time comes to start off.

Turning to the right from the nearside lane or to the left from the offside lane is inexcusably bad driving, but it happens all too frequently. Under such circumstances it is better to be 'safe' than to be 'in the right'.

Cultivate 'defensive' driving in your own interests. To insist implacably on your rights is a dangerous philosophy when driving.

Try to position your car so as to observe the braking lights of vehicles which are ahead of the one immediately in front of you, but without driving in echelon.

It might be necessary to pull out slightly to get a view of the road ahead before overtaking. If you decide not to overtake, however, return immediately to your nearside.

If your side of the road is obstructed by road works or parked vehicles, give way to oncoming traffic.

Do not overtake at the approach to pedestrian crossings, road junctions, humpback bridges, or where the road narrows. If you are likely to inconvenience or endanger other road users, hold back.

Many motorists avoid accidents only as a result of the courtesy and good driving of others.

Drive your own car, and let the other man drive his; if he is determined to exceed the speed limit don't try to baulk him. It's *his* driving licence, remember.

Drive up to the permitted speed where it is safe to do so; those who hog the crown of the road at speeds well below the legal maximum for their own selfish reasons and nothing else create a nuisance.

They may claim to have avoided accidents, but may well have *caused* many.

The greatest danger on our roads is the incompetent driver, whose driving lacks not only system but a basic knowledge of technique.

You will see him level with a lorry, trying to overtake in the wrong gear, usually at the approach to a bend. The lorry driver is faced with the choice of braking to let him in or imperilling any traffic which might be approaching.

Such drivers might claim that they 'never drive fast' ... but how 'fast' is dangerous?

If you follow a first-class driver, you will be able to anticipate his every move by the position of his car on the road.

His braking lights will appear in time to give adequate warning of an impending hazard, and intelligent use of the trafficators will practically eliminate the need for arm signals.

His driving is smooth and *progressive*, but never hurried.

Arrogant, aggressive drivers are without exception incompetent drivers, and there is no place for them on our overcrowded roads.

XX

DRIVING ON THE MOTORWAYS

MANY people, even including experienced motorists, dislike driving on the motorways. Presumably their main reason is the speed at which vehicles, both private and commercial, travel.

Now, motorways are what their name implies—roads which give drivers every facility for travelling fast, with the assurance that they will not have to cope with pedestrians, cyclists, moped riders, learners, invalid carriages and animals.

Since there are no acute bends, cross-roads, roundabouts or traffic lights, all that is required is everyday driving skill and commonsense, which is no more than should be applied in any circumstances.

If you own a family saloon which normally would be driven at speeds below say 50 m.p.h., don't expect to be able to drive it flat out for miles on end on a motorway without some sort of trouble.

It will be necessary to ensure that your vehicle is in fully serviceable condition. Do not maintain high speeds on worn tyres. Make sure that their pressures are as recommended by the manufacturers for fast driving.

Check the fan belt; many breakdowns result from overheating as a result of this breaking under the strain of high-speed motoring, or being too slack to drive the water pump and fan. The dynamo and battery may also suffer from a defective fan belt.

Keep an eye on the ammeter, temperature and oil gauges, or their equivalent warning lights. If any indicate trouble, either drive in the slow lane until you can pull off the motorway at one of the authorised exit places, or if there seems imminent danger you would be justified in stopping on the hard shoulder to investigate.

If you breakdown, pull (or push) your car on to the hard shoulder, and *never* walk on the motorway or let your passengers do so.

Strict lane discipline is imperative when driving on the motorways. Always follow the advice given in the Highway Code, as follows:
On a two-lane motorway keep to the inside lane except when overtaking; on a three-lane motorway the inside one is for slow-moving traffic, the middle lane for faster-moving vehicles and the outside lane for overtaking (Note.—A goods vehicle with an unladen weight of more than 3 tons, or *any* vehicle drawing a trailer, may not use the outside lane of a three-lane carriageway, unless there are exceptional circumstances).

Overtake *only* on the right. **Never change lanes until you have first checked your mirror(s) and blind spot, and signal your intention clearly and in good time. Make sure that the lane you will enter is clear far enough behind and ahead. Be particularly careful about this at dusk, or in fog or mist.**

Remember that, difficult though it is to assess the speed of an approaching vehicle, it is almost impossible to assess, accurately, the speed of a vehicle coming up from the rear. If in doubt, always play safe and let it pass before pulling out to overtake.

To reduce monotony vary your speed now and again, keep the car well ventilated and, should you be overcome by tiredness, leave the motorway for a rest. Never pull up on the hard shoulder (except in case of breakdown).

If you drive fast for a long period you may lose all sense of speed. It will be necessary to re-adjust yourself by reference to the speedometer when quitting the motorway.

Drive your car at the cruising speed for which it was designed, and of course within legal speed limits.

If there is a strong crosswind, make allowance as you enter and leave the shelter of bridges and cuttings, and don't be taken by surprise.

Obey police signs absolutely. If you should breakdown, try to ascertain which way the nearest telephone lies (this can generally be seen by the furlong mark or posts) and walk to it to summon assistance.

Motorways have been so designed that traffic can join them without risk if drivers follow the advice given in Paragraph 107 of the Highway Code, which reads as follows: 'When you join a motorway other than at its start, you will approach a from road on the left (a slip road). Give way to traffic already on the motorway. Watch for a safe gap in the traffic in the inside lane on the motorway, and then accelerate in the extra lane (the acceleration lane) so that when you join the inside lane you are already travelling at the same speed as the traffic on it.'

Before going on to a motorway always check your petrol, oil and water; driving at prolonged high speed uses up petrol faster, while to run short of oil or water is productive of expensive noises from the engine.

When you reach the end of the motorway, remember you are returning on to slow, congested roads, so be prepared to exercise tolerance and restraint on your speed, as at first you will seem to be going painfully slow.

XXI

GEARS. THEIR USE AND ABUSE

THE theme of this manual is mastery of the vehicle, at all times and under all conditions. A driver who is unskilled or unpractised in the use of every control when the vehicle is in motion is not in complete command of it.

As part of the Advanced Driving Test, drivers of manually-operated-gear cars are asked to change up and down through all the gears competently and smoothly, with the car in motion.

This is not a gimmick, but to prove that, in the event of brake failure, the vehicle could be kept under control; also that, when climbing a steep hill, the driver would not have to stop his car in order to engage first gear.

The reasons for fitting a gearbox to a car can be described simply as (1) to maintain engine revolutions in relation to the car's speed, (2) to provide a neutral position for use when the vehicle is stationary, and (3) to provide a means of reversing the vehicle.

Numbers two and three are so obvious that they require no further explanation; number one, however, is not always clearly understood.

The higher gears permit the driver to increase the car's speed without an appreciable increase of engine revolutions.

The lower gears enable him to start easily and negotiate hills without effort, by increasing engine revs. at the expense of road speed.

Those who learned to drive on vehicles fitted with 'crash' (i.e., non-synchromesh) gearboxes know that it was essential to double de-clutch in order to change gear smoothly and without grating noises.

On modern cars fitted with synchromesh gears, it is not strictly necessary to double de-clutch in order to change quietly and smoothly, because a built-in device brings the gear wheels to a matching speed before their teeth come into engagement.

Double de-clutching is essential, however, when changing into a non-synchronised first gear. Even where all the gears have synchromesh, many drivers still use the double de-clutching technique.

(Note: It would appear that there are differences of opinion, even between car manufacturers, in connection with this. Some say it is desirable, others that it merely increases wear on clutch withdrawal mechanism).

Drivers who double de-clutch proficiently, however, never experience difficulty in changing gears smoothly on any type of car fitted with a manually-operated gearbox.

For those who would like to practise double de-clutching this is how it is done:—

CHANGING UP

Push clutch out, take foot off accelerator pedal.
Slip gear lever into neutral, let clutch in.
Push clutch out again and push gear lever into next higher gear position.

Let clutch in and apply acceleration simultaneously with taking up the drive.

CHANGING DOWN

When changing down it is necessary to adapt the engine revolutions to the lower gear ratio, and this is done by holding the right foot perfectly still on the accelerator pedal, while pushing the clutch out. Now slip gear lever into neutral position, let the clutch in for a moment (the engine revving up as the load is removed), then press it out again and move gear lever into the lower gear position. Let the clutch in and the car will proceed smoothly. But don't let the engine 'race' during the operation.

The most difficult part of this operation is to hold the accelerator perfectly still (some drivers 'blip' the pedal when in neutral instead). When you have mastered it the change of gear is imperceptible.

It is the ability to drive in complete sympathy with his car which makes the polished driver. He changes gears by sound and feel—gently and never forcefully—and does not have to be reminded by a labouring engine that a change down is overdue. There is a maximum road speed for each gear (usually mentioned in the instruction manual), and no attempt should be made to change into a lower gear at a speed exceeding this, or engine revs. may mount dangerously.

From the point of view of the Advanced Driving Test, correct gear selection and using the gears to fullest advantage is more important than the actual technique used for changing them. While acceleration will often get you out of trouble, it is necessary to remember that this power is only at your command when the correct gear is engaged.

Overtaking should always be carried out in the shortest distance consistent with safety. If you have to trundle along by the side of the vehicle you are overtaking, with the accelerator pedal pressed right down to the floor, you are either in the wrong gear or you should not have attempted to overtake at all.

Coasting downhill in neutral in order to save a small amount of petrol is not regarded as good driving practice, for the reason that it would be impossible to accelerate out of an emergency.

Like everything else connected with driving, we have to keep a sense of proportion. Excessive gear changing should be avoided, because it could be interpreted as a sign of indecision.

When a car is fitted with automatic transmission, there is obviously no actual changing of gears to be done by the driver. At the same time, however, there *are* different ratios and it is possible for a skilful driver to use the accelerator pedal in such a manner as to minimise any jerk which can occur when the automatic mechanism makes the change. This transmission is dealt with in the next chapter.

XXII

AUTOMATIC TRANSMISSION

DYED-IN-THE-WOOL drivers are sometimes heard to remark 'Like driving a dodgem car at the fair', in reference to the skill required to drive a car with automatic transmission.

Now, while it is fair to say that any intelligent driver can make an automatic car 'go', to handle it really skilfully is another matter.

The expert driver is naturally proud of being able to change gears manually, whether or not fitted with synchromesh, noiselessly, smoothly and without effort.

The end result is the same, however, whether auto or manual transmission is fitted. The car should move smoothly and the passengers be unaware by any jerking that a change of gear has taken place.

As has already been said, the accelerator should be treated as an instrument, not merely a pedal, and this applies equally when driving with auto as with manual change.

Various systems of automatic transmission are available, and (as has already been said) they vary in the number of ratios they offer. It is not necessarily cost which governs this, but the nature of the car itself.

The only infinitely variable transmission is on the Dutch-built DAF. This has twin belts of 'V' type, which are automatically caused to raise and lower themselves in adjustable pulleys, thus varying the ratio between engine and back wheels.

All other auto transmissions have a 'fluid coupling', which acts in similar fashion to the normal clutch, and the drive is transmitted through a gearbox to the wheels. The gears are usually of a different pattern to those of an ordinary gearbox, being 'epicyclic'. They are in constant mesh, and were, in fact, used on the old model T ('Tin Lizzie') Ford half a century ago. Even then they were no novelty.

The actual changing of gears is effected by means of a control system which acts in combination with devices operated by (a) the effort which the engine is exerting, i.e., the amount of 'suction' in the induction pipe, (b) the speed at which the engine is revolving and (c) throttle opening.

Thus, when the car is running easily on level roads under light load, the controls act to engage top gear. When accelerating or climbing a hill, they will bring a lower gear into action. When the car comes to a standstill they engage bottom (or second) gear ready for a restart, which the driver does by merely depressing the accelerator pedal.

Most systems have an overriding control, whereby the driver can engage a lower gear, and/or hold it, if he considers it desirable. For instance, when descending a steep hill, or when climbing a twisty one, top gear would otherwise automatically engage as the throttle was eased. On a hairpin bend, when climbing, say, a mountain pass, this would be a nuisance and even dangerous.

Alternatively, if maximum acceleration is required when overtaking, or in emergency, most automatic transmissions have a 'kick down' change operated by pressing the accelerator to the floorboard. This instantly brings a lower gear into use.

On becoming the owner of an automatic transmission car, one should take it to a quiet district and familiarise oneself with the speeds at which the gears change; these vary according to whether one is using light or full throttle.

When starting from cold and employing the choke, which makes the engine run at fast idling speed, be very careful that the hand brake is firmly on when moving the selector from

77

neutral to forward drive or reverse. The torque converter ('clutch' hydraulic) causes the car to 'creep' unless this is done. This same creep can be useful when reversing into a parking space, utilising the brake instead of, as one would with a normal clutch, light footwork on accelerator and clutch pedal.

Automatic transmission can also be helpful if one has got the car bogged down, or stuck in a snow patch, by keeping the engine running at fast idling speed and alternately moving the selector lever between forward and reverse positions. But *never* attempt to engage reverse when the car is travelling forward at anything more than a crawl.

In the event of breakdown, a car with auto transmission may be damaged if it is towed without expert knowledge. This is because the gearbox is lubricated by an oil pump driven from its engine end, and if this is not working—as when engine failure is the cause of the breakdown—lack of lubrication is liable to cause a seizure in the gearbox. The makers' handbook will contain information about the particular car concerned, and should be carefully studied.

Most automatic transmissions have an overriding control which can be operated manually by the driver when he wants to hold a lower gear. The makers' handbook should be carefully studied so that the most intelligent use can be made of the automatic box in securing the best out of the car.

When a 'P' position is given on the selector quadrant, this is to lock the transmission when the car is parked. It must *only* be engaged when the car is stationary, and is about equivalent to leaving a car fitted with manual gearbox with, say, bottom gear engaged.

XXIII

KEEPING THE CAR SAFE

A N advanced motorist will do his utmost to maintain his car in thoroughly safe condition. At the first hint of anything unusual developing he will trace the cause and either rectify it himself or have his garage do so with the least possible delay.

A driver must therefore constantly maintain a state of alertness to detect any deterioration, gradual or sudden, in a vehicle's condition and performance.

A not uncommon trouble is for wheel nuts to loosen themselves, if after a wheel has been changed the requisite degree of tightening of all wheel nuts has not been checked. This might reveal itself by a curious sound developing, or by a steering 'wander' setting in. If a wheel *does* come off when the car is in motion the result can be dangerous in the extreme, and not only to those in the actual car concerned.

The steering gear itself is, of course, one of the most vital parts of the car. Should any change in its normal operation be noticed, instant attention must be given. There are so many joints and bearings involved that it is usually work for an expert mechanic to trace and rectify the source of trouble.

With a front wheel drive car, the owner should occasionally drive it round on full lock in a tight circle and listen for any clicking sounds which might denote undue wear or perhaps the breakage of a part in the constant velocity joints between the drive shafts and the wheels.

The braking system is also, of course, something the owner must keep under constant surveillance. If hard application causes the car to pull either to right or left, immediate attention must be paid to adjustment and balance. This is a thing that owners should not attempt to do themselves, on a 'hit or miss' basis, but for a properly equipped service station.

Brake operation on the modern car is generally a complicated matter, utilising hydraulic application and/or servo systems. Unskilled adjustments may even result in the brakes developing really dangerous characteristics when applied, especially with what is termed 'panic' pressure.

The majority of roadside breakdowns attributable to engine failure arise from one or other of the following causes:—

1. Lack of petrol in the tank.

2. Dirt or water in the tank, which is drawn through the feed pipe when the level of fuel in the tank gets low, and collecting in the fuel pump or carburettor.

3. A gas-lock in the fuel pipe line, sometimes caused by heat from the engine if the petrol pipe runs close to it.

4. Ignition failure through a wire detaching itself from the coil or distributor, or chafing through and causing a short circuit.

5. One or more of the high tension leads jumping off the plug terminal (this would cause only the cylinder(s) affected to go out of action).

6. A defect inside the coil (many motorists, especially when taking their cars abroad, carry a spare coil).

7. A defect inside the distributor, possibly the contact points becoming loosened and having closed themselves together, or a crack in the distributor casing.

8. A spark plug or plugs sooting up, perhaps through an excess of oil in the sump and loose pistons. An unsuitable type of plug can soot up if the engine idles too much, e.g., a racing type plug in a touring car used largely in traffic.

9. A sticking valve, possibly caused through an unsuitable upper cylinder lubricant having been put in the petrol, or an excessive amount of it.

Tyres, their condition and pressure, are obviously a major factor in a car's safety. An advanced motorist will always have a reliable pressure gauge on his car or in his garage, and make frequent use of it, checking all five wheels (i.e., including the spare). He will also see that his jack is kept in satisfactory working condition.

Driving on motorways involves a greater strain on tyres than do the ordinary roads on which frequent slowing down is necessary. Heat builds up with sustained high speed due to the increased amount of flexing of the side walls, and if the pressure is below the maker's recommended figure this will cause serious trouble eventually.

In buying a new tyre or tyres, if much motorway driving is normally done, care should be exercised to see that the right type is purchased for the speeds envisaged. Never mix 'radial ply' and 'cross ply' on the same axle: danger can ensue. Consult a reputable dealer when replacing tyres.

XXIV

MASTERY OVER MECHANISM

A DRIVER who is the complete master of his vehicle's machinery can make it conform to his requirements. This does not necessarily mean that he is a mechanic, but that he understands sufficient about the mechanism to realise the whys and wherefores of its controls.

The movement of his feet and hands will be instinctively correct under all conditions of driving, even in emergency. He will not have to feel for the brake pedal or grope for the gearlever.

He will know to a close degree of accuracy how his car or vehicle will behave on varying conditions of road surface and at different speeds. He will have tested its reaction to emergency application of the brakes and to sudden swerving.

His use of clutch and gear controls will be smooth and jerk-free, and under normal circumstances deceleration will be steady and progressive, with due regard to following vehicles.

If bottom gear is not equipped with synchromesh he will master the technique of double de-clutching to enable that gear to be engaged with the car moving slowly.

He will know the width of his car and be able to judge from a reasonable distance whether he can steer it cleanly through a constricted passage.

Similarly, the length of car ahead of the driving seat will have been checked by practice so that garaging or parking is made certain without bumping any wall or vehicle in front.

Reversing into a confined parking space will also have been perfected by practice until the car can be manoeuvred with certainty.

XXV

CAR 'SYMPATHY'

To be an advanced driver does not mean that one must be a skilled mechanic or an expert in car design and construction.

It does, however, entail one having a basic knowledge of the way in which the mechanism functions, so that it can be handled with a degree of sympathy from the driving seat. It is also desirable to know sufficient to ensure that the working parts are in a safe condition and to detect likely causes of breakdown.

Without going deeply into technical matters, a run through the major components of a car and the best methods of keeping them in good humour may be helpful to some readers.

First and foremost, the whys and wherefores of the internal combustion engine should be reasonably well understood. And, since very nearly all car engines today are of the piston-in-cylinder type, we will concentrate on them.

Inside the cylinders—there may be two, three, four, six or more of them—a piston is caused to move up and down or horizontally back and forth and a connecting rod coupled to the engine's mainshaft (crankshaft) by what is called a big-end bearing causes the shaft to rotate.

Like the various other bearings, this needs continual lubrication. It receives oil from a force pump which draws it from a well in the base chamber ('sump') into which the oil runs when topping-up takes place. If at any time topping-up is neglected and the engine runs dry of oil, or even too low, 'seizure' (locking up solid) may occur, with consequent loss of car control.

The correct level of oil that should be in the engine's sump is marked on the dipstick, and when this is pulled out the actual level is readily seen. There is also a second marker near the bottom end of the dipstick; this is the danger point and immediate topping-up is necessary. At the same time, there is nothing to be gained by filling to above the top mark; in fact this may allow leakage from the engine or loss of power by churning. Obey the dipstick marks carefully, therefore.

The engine runs and develops power because a mixture of petrol vapour and air is sucked into the cylinders by the downward or horizontal motion of the pistons. Each cylinder receives its charge in turn through an inlet valve, which stays open while its piston is sucking but closes when the cylinder has taken in its charge.

Now the piston is at the end of its stroke and reverses its motion, but the charge of gas cannot find any escape and therefore becomes highly compressed at the other end of the piston's stroke (called 'top dead centre').

Here it should be interposed that the mixture of petrol vapour and air has been concocted inside the carburettor, an instrument which is fed with petrol from the tank via a supply pipe line and a small pump driven either electrically or by mechanical means from the engine.

As petrol is highly inflammable, but not explosive until a suitable quota of oxygen has been mixed with its vapour, the meaning of the word carburettor becomes clear ('the apparatus for impregnating air with fine particles of fuel and thus preparing the explosive mixture for the cylinders', says the dictionary).

Returning to the highly compressed charge in the cylinder, it is obviously in a very combustible state indeed, and, as the piston is now at or near top dead centre, the act of firing it will drive the piston downwards with great force.

The combustion is caused by an electric spark at the points of a plug screwed into the cylinder head, and is produced by a special coil which transforms the 12 volts (or sometimes 6) generated by the car's electrical equipment into a very high voltage ('high tension') current capable of jumping the gap between the points of the sparking plug.

In order that the spark shall occur in the right cylinder at the right instant, this current is directed to each one in turn by a 'distributor', rotated by the engine.

Having expended its force in driving down the piston, the burnt charge has to be got rid of, and so an exhaust valve is now caused to open and to remain open while the piston makes its way back up the cylinder. The exhaust gas is expelled therefrom along a pipe which sends it out into the atmosphere after allowing it to expand inside a chamber known as a silencer or muffler.

Each cylinder in turn goes through this routine of four strokes of its piston (two up and two down) to complete the process of drawing in the explosive charge, compressing it, exploding and exhausting it. This occupies two revolutions of the engine's crank shaft, during which there is only the one power impulse. This is the cycle of operations of the four-stroke engine, such as is fitted to the overwhelming proportion of cars.

A comparatively small number (mostly of foreign origin) have what are known as two-stroke engines, in which the above mentioned four separate strokes of the piston are telescoped into two. This is effected by utilising the crank chamber as an auxiliary compartment for compression purposes, and making apertures cut in the cylinder walls take the place of normal valves. Small motor-cycle and industrial engines in particular make use of the two-stroke principle, which works well on them but has certain inherent drawbacks for cars, mainly concerned with uneven slow running and smoke emission from the exhaust pipe.

It has to be borne in mind that all petrol engines develop only a small proportion of their full power when they are running slowly. On the average, they have to be turning over at some 4,000 revolutions per minute, and sometimes more, before the *maximum* power of which they are capable is developed; this may represent, on top gear, a road speed of perhaps 60 miles per hour.

Maximum power is not everything, however: equally important to the driver is the engine speed at which it develops maximum *torque*, or pulling power. This is usually quoted in terms of 'pounds feet' and indicates the ability of the engine to exert its strongest tractive effort (pushing the car along) at a speed generally (in the case of a touring car) about two-thirds that at which maximum *horse-power* is developed.

To quote a fairly typical case: The engine of a certain popular car will develop 84 brake-horse-power (called 'brake' because it is measured on a test bench where an exact braking force can be applied and calibrated by electrical or hydraulic means) at 5,300 r.p.m. Its maximum torque, however, is developed at only 2,100 r.p.m., when it is 99 lb. ft.

This means that, as an engine speed of 1,000 r.p.m. on this particular car's top gear gives about 16½ m.p.h. road speed, the car's ability to surmount hills will be at its best at 2.1 x 16.4= 34.4 m.p.h. In other words, it is a car that should suit the type of driver who is not too enthusiastic about gear-changing, although, of course, this is not the maximum speed at which the car will climb.

The very nature of a car engine does, however, demand that varying its rate of revolution in relation to the road speed is an essential. Once an engine starts to labour it will be sending 'judders' through the transmission which do no good to any part of the car.

An advanced driver will sense just when the next lower gear will allow the engine to 'rev' freely and be ready to accelerate without hesitation when the throttle (or accelerator) pedal is pressed. Also, to anticipate when a change of gear will be made. And, although no mention was made of this particular control (accelerator or throttle) when the carburettor was being discussed, it is, of course, a most important one where sympathetic driving is concerned. Its action is to open and close the valve in the induction pipe (connecting carburettor with engine), at the same time regulating the proportionate volumes of petrol vapour and air which keep the mixture at its most efficient.

Here let it be mentioned that this latter is a complicated process, and that expert 'tuning' of the carburettor can often
improve a car's performance. The proportion of air to petrol
vapour desirable for best possible combustion is about 14 to 1,
but this would not suit every phase of an engine's running, from
pulling hard up a hill to running lightly loaded on the level or
downhill.

Consequently, a carburettor has to do its best to cope with a
multitude of conditions, not the least of which is to make the
engine an easy starter from cold, for which a strong (i.e.,
petrol-rich) mixture is required. A control known as the choke
has to be introduced to achieve this, and it may be under the
driver's manual operation or automatically worked through a
thermostat.

It can be very detrimental to the interior of an engine if the
choke is left too long in operation. An over-rich mixture will
tend to swamp the cylinder walls with petrol and to denude
them of their protecting film of oil.

When starting up from cold, therefore, keep the choke in use
for the least possible time, i.e., until the engine 'picks up'
readily. Do not let it go on idling for any length of time, but
get the car under way at a reasonable speed with the least
avoidable delay. It is when starting up in the morning that dry
and cold cylinder walls are liable to receive the greatest harm
and the best prevention is to get an oil film delivered to them
quickly.

Even the most sophisticated carburettor cannot be expected to
provide a perfect petrol vapour/air mixture at every throttle
opening, and so methods of *injecting* a metered amount of fuel
into the cylinders or induction ports are receiving close attention from makers of racing cars and the more expensive types
of touring cars. Production costs are likely to rule petrol in-
jection out of the 'popular' car market for some time to come,
however.

In the matter of transmission, the position of manual gearchange
is being more and more threatened by the increasing popularity
of the automatically operated gearbox. Many drivers who have

grown accustomed to this insist that they would never return to the gear lever.

Advanced drivers are naturally divided in their loyalties, but the fact remains that automatic transmission is making steady progress. It certainly assists car sympathy, for engine labouring is avoided and, whatever the driver does, the correct gear is waiting for him when he next presses the accelerator pedal. He also has an overriding control which enables him to make an instant change down for overtaking.

An automatic transmission can have four, three or even only two actual gear ratios, but an essential feature of it is either a hydraulic coupling or torque converter. This makes use of oil as a means of transmitting the drive from engine to gearbox, in somewhat similar style to a water or steam turbine's vanes.

A torque converter is, in fact, capable of acting as an infinitely-variable-ratio gear of itself. To use it as such, however, is wasteful of engine power and may be productive of excessive heat from the liquid medium.

Most automatic transmissions on British cars have three ratios of gearing, some with a selector which eliminates bottom gear for starting off on level ground. The smallest car of all, BMC's Automatic Mini, has four ratios, to prevent too much work being thrown on the torque converter. Britain's most expensive car, the Rolls-Royce, also has four ratios, but in this case to give the utmost smoothness in changing. Two-speed automatic transmissions are mainly confined to big-engined cars, Americans especially, where there is only occasional need for anything but high gear in conjunction with a torque converter.

Manually operated gearboxes require a clutch which, although capable of being slipped to a limited degree for starting away from rest, gives a solid, positive drive from the engine, through the selected gear, to the road wheels. It usually consists of three flat-faced discs, the centre one being faced with friction material, which are pressed into firm contact by a spring or springs. Use of the clutch pedal breaks the contact, disconnects engine from transmission and allows the gear lever to be moved.

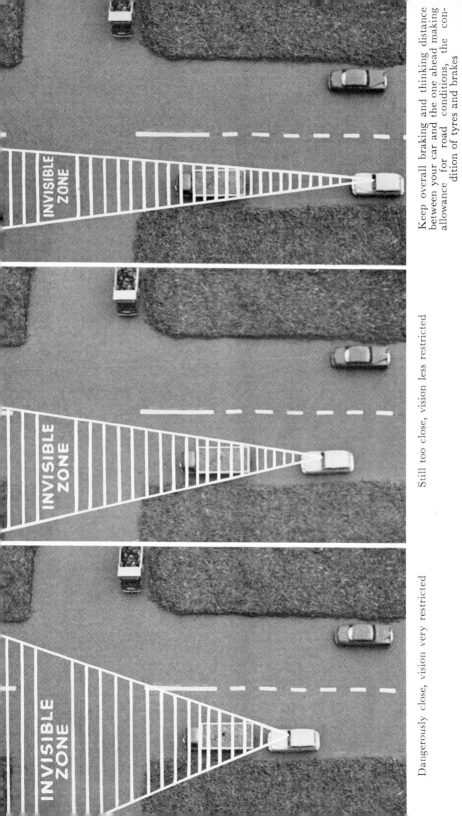

INVISIBLE ZONE

INVISIBLE ZONE

INVISIBLE ZONE

Dangerously close, vision very restricted

Still too close, vision less restricted

Keep overall braking and thinking distance between your car and the one ahead making allowance for road conditions, the condition of tyres and brakes

◀ 1

Pull level with the car
in front, leaving 18″ to
2′ 0″ clearance

◀ 2

Full left lock and slowly
back until the rear of the
foremost car is
approximately level with
your windscreen pillar

ghten the front wheels
ᴵ continue reversing
you are sure that your
 bumper will clear the
ᴿ of the car in front

◀ 4

Full right lock and
continue in reverse until
you are parked behind the
front vehicle

◀ 5

One move forward to
centralise your car and
leave room to enable you to
get your car out and for
the driver behind you to get
out without damaging
your car

Above: Universal trainer and reaction tester, by courtesy of RoSPA House

Below: Testing recovery from glare, by courtesy of RoSPA House

The fitting of synchromesh has robbed gearchanging of most of its former difficulties by introducing synchronising surfaces which make the gearwheels adjust to one another's speed before being brought into contact. Some cars still do not have synchromesh to bottom gear, however, and then the driver has to master the art of double de-clutching if he wants to engage that gear with the car on the move, albeit slowly (see page 73).

To practise double de-clutching, the car should be driven in bottom gear at 10–12 m.p.h. and the sound of the engine's revolutions memorised. Now change up to second, but continue to keep the speedometer needle at the same figure, and again memorise the engine's r.p.m. note. It will obviously be lower, because there is usually a pronounced gap between the two gears in their relation between engine and road wheels.

To take a common example, bottom may be $13\frac{3}{4}$ revolutions of the engine to one of the road wheels, and 2nd $9\frac{1}{4}$ to 1. It is accordingly necessary to raise the engine's speed by some 50 per cent, or half as much again, if the gears are to mesh without protest when the change is made. Practice will probably be needed in order to make perfect change-downs every time.

Earlier in this chapter reference was made to the compression of the petrol/air charge before it was fired by the electric spark, but the exact degree of compression was not touched on. There is, in fact, no hard and fast rule about this, for an engine designer arranges it to suit the purpose in mind.

Naturally, the higher the ratio of compression (within limits) the greater will be the force of the combustion, but this is not an unmixed blessing. For a racing car with comparatively little weight, suitable fuel and an expert driver, high revolutions are of primary importance because five or six gear ratios have been specially arranged to suit the topography of a given race circuit. The highest ratio of compression that will just avoid detonation will probably be given in such cases.

Detonation is self-explosion, or premature firing of the charge before the spark occurs. It can be held back by the use of special fuels, but these would not be generally available to the ordinary motorist for everyday purposes, or too expensive.

Hence the compression ratio of the average touring car's engine is fixed at a figure usually varying between 8 and 9 to 1. A sports model engine may go up to 11 to 1, and there is a continual tendency towards putting up maximum horse-power by raising the compression ratio.

This does involve the use of the more expensive grades of petrol, because detonation will be likely to set in as the combustion chamber begins to acquire a coating of carbon inside. In any case, knocking or 'pinking' will force the owner to buy the dearest petrol after a while and he may well wonder whether the extra cost of high compression ratios is justified.

Here it may be pointed out that there is no merit in buying a more expensive grade of petrol than an engine actually requires. If it runs well and knock-free on 'ordinary' grade, there is nothing to be gained by using premium; similarly 100-octane fuel is no advantage if premium satisfies the engine's requirements. The costlier petrol is not more 'powerful', nor will it give more miles per gallon.

Octane rating is not of itself a measure of quality, but merely a calibration of the suitability of a particular fuel to a given engine. A low compression (say about 7 to 1 ratio) engine may well be satisfied with cheap—'ordinary' grade—petrol. On the other hand, a sports model engine will perhaps knock very readily unless given 100-octane petrol, and knocking is detrimental to bearings in time. Most modern family saloons with engines of about 8.3 to 9 to 1 compression ratio find premium grade petrol (say 95 octane) perfectly satisfactory.

As regards lubricants, it is highly desirable to follow the car maker's recommendations, since different brands of oil have various additives and some may suit a given engine better than others. It is best not to mix different brands by topping up with an oil other than that which is already in the sump.

The lubricant is an engine's very 'life blood': an insufficiency or the use of low quality, unbranded oil sold at cut prices may prove a very expensive economy indeed. Check level regularly, and especially after long runs at high speed.

Also, keep a careful watch on the level of liquid in the battery. During hot weather, and particularly if you have driven hard and fast (and all the more if the battery is housed under the bonnet), see to it that the electrolyte (liquid) keeps the plates inside the battery always covered. Replenish with distilled water only. Keep careful check, too, on the level of the hydraulic brake fluid.

XXVI

PRIORITIES

In the U.K. there is no basic priority rule, and for this reason priority where necessary has to be marked by STOP or GIVE WAY signs. These already exist at many junctions and they will be placed as soon as possible at all junctions throughout the country, though at the less heavily trafficked junctions GIVE WAY will be indicated by carriageway markings only.

Until this is done, however, the basic rule at all unsigned junctions is that drivers on both roads must take all necessary precautions to avoid accidents. Subject to this it is reasonable that drivers on main roads should to a greater extent rely on drivers from minor roads giving way to them. But they have no absolute legal right to precedence since, in the absence of signs, it is by no means always obvious which is the major and which is the minor road.

Therefore, where there are not signs at a junction, drivers on both roads must be on their guard. Unsigned junctions are likely to occur less frequently on trunk and classified than on unclassified roads.

The STOP sign means that the driver must stop in all circumstances, and an offence is committed if a driver does not come to a full stop at the appropriate line. It is because STOP signs are put only at junctions with dangerously bad visibility that this absolute regulation is necessary.

The STOP sign, however, has a second and equally important meaning. It gives the injunction also that the driver, having stopped, should then give way to traffic on the road he intends to enter.

At junctions where there is good visibility from the minor road, GIVE WAY signs are used instead of STOP signs, and at these signs stopping is not obligatory.

The meaning of GIVE WAY in both cases is that the driver entering the major road shall proceed so as not to endanger any vehicle on the major road, or cause it to change its speed or course in order to avoid an accident.

An advanced driver will act defensively at all unsigned junctions by reducing speed so that he can stop if necessary within the limits of his vision. To this precaution can be added the use of a horn in specially dangerous circumstances and the flashing of headlamps after dark.

Since many motorists take their cars abroad, it may be of interest to quote from an official pamphlet issued for the guidance of foreigners visiting France (where road laws are explicit and strongly enforced).

'A solid yellow line in the centre of the road must never be crossed or overridden. A broken yellow line may be crossed for the purpose of overtaking another vehicle or of crossing the road. Double lines must not be crossed except when the broken line is nearest to the driver's left-hand side.

'The driver who has to pull away from the side of the road on starting off, or has to slow down, stop, or change direction, must first of all make sure that he may do so without danger to himself or other road users. He must signal his intentions a sufficient time in advance.

'In all built-up areas vehicles may not exceed 60 kilometres per hour (37 m.p.h.). Some urban areas have a lower speed limit than this, which is indicated at the point where it comes into force.

'Outside urban areas, speed is restricted only where road signs indicate this fact, together with the limit imposed. This does not relieve a driver of the duty of driving with caution, or of adjusting his speed to visibility or other conditions calling for a reduction in speed, even though he may have priority.

'In particular, speed should always be reduced at crossroads, on bends, at hilltops and wherever the road is used by pedestrians.

'Outside urban areas, drivers on trunk roads have right of way, as well as on others where this right is indicated on road signs bearing the words *Passage Protégé* (this shows there are Halt signs on the side roads). Trunk roads are legally declared as such (*Routes à Grande Circulation*).

'Warning signs similar to those of *passage protégé* are also used to warn drivers who will NOT have right of way that they are approaching trunk roads. Other than on priority roads as described above, when two vehicles meet at a crossroads, the one on the left of the other must give way.

'In Paris and the Département of the Seine, drivers must park on the right-hand side of the road in the direction the car is travelling. Only in one-way streets is left-hand side parking permitted.

'Sound your horn only in case of real need. In Paris and some other cities and towns the use of the horn is forbidden except in case of urgent danger. A sign showing a horn with a cancellation bar through it is displayed at the entrance of these places. During the night, headlight signals replace audible warning.

'It is an offence to dazzle other drivers. Amber headlights are obligatory for French drivers, and it is strongly recommended that those coming from other countries where white lights are still used should conform to the French custom. Between sunset and dawn and at other times of bad visibility, stationary vehicles must show a clearly visible light to front and rear, on that side of the vehicle which is nearest to the centre of the road. This rule does not apply in Paris and the Département of the Seine (also some other localities) provided that the vehicle is clearly visible by other means such as street lighting for a distance of 110 yards.'

Somewhat similar regulations apply in other Continental countries (excepting the use of amber-coloured headlamps). Priority to vehicles on one's right is a well established rule in countries where traffic keeps to the right.

In some countries the fact that one is driving on a main trunk road is denoted by small oblong signs erected at intervals, but the priority these confer in the open country is shown to cease at the entrance to built-up areas by a similar sign with a cancellation bar through it. Towns in, for instance, Germany have priority signs at even the most minor street crossings.

XXVII

WHAT IS 'ADVANCED' DRIVING?

COURTENAY EDWARDS, *the well known motoring writer, interviewed* GEORGE EYLES, *Director of Tests of the I.A.M., on an enquiry which has often been put to him by readers.*

COURTENAY EDWARDS: Tell me, please, what you mean by 'advanced' driving? As you know, I passed my I.A.M. test many years ago, and yet I find it difficult sometimes to tell my readers exactly what the phrase means. And, of course, there are so many false stories passed around that I'd like to hear from your own lips an accurate description of it.

GEORGE EYLES: In a few words, I think I would say that Advanced Driving is a state of mind, plus technical competence, well-developed powers of observation and a healthy imagination which gives a driver a sense of keen anticipation of the unexpected.

C. E.: Do you, then, expect an advanced driver to crawl around the roads, looking here, there and everywhere in case trouble arises?

G. E.: Certainly not crawl. An advanced driver can travel from A to B as fast as anyone, but he will do so with safety under all conditions, and without endangering or frightening his passengers or any other road users. He may drive fast but he will never permit his journey to degenerate into a race against the clock. His state of mind will be such that all the time he is at the wheel he will be concentrating on his driving and realising that it is a whole time job.

96

C. E.: Is not this a counsel of perfection? What does the advanced driver do if he is obstructed by a crown-of-the-road crawler—or, alternatively, if he is overtaken by another driver whom he considers to be 'carving him up'?

G. E.: He may certainly be annoyed, but his state of mind should prevent his temper getting the better of him to the extent that he takes unnecessary risks. Neither does he retaliate or threaten the other man with violence, as I believe has been known to happen. Drivers who actually resort to physical violence should be banned from the roads altogether.

C. E.: What are your views about observing speed limits? I seem to remember reading a little while ago that advanced drivers who keep their speed down in restricted areas to the legal limit are 'conspicuous and a nuisance to other people'.

G. E.: There does appear to be a widespread idea that speed limit signs possess no meaning, and have no legal significance. The same goes for Stop and Give Way signs. Presumably so long as nearly everyone who flouts such signs gets away with it, the Grand Prix spirit will continue to flourish. At the same time, the thought that a driving licence can now be lost very easily if police activity should be intensified does, I hope, encourage the advanced motorist to pay respect to the law of the land. We may all feel, perhaps, that in some places speed limits have been applied unintelligently, but that is no excuse for the apparent belief that a motorist can be his own judge of what is and what is not an unjustifiable speed.

C. E.: As the Institute's Director of Tests, you have a staff of more than 20 whole time Examiners under you up and down the country. Would you tell me what you, and they, look for when conducting a test? And is the attitude of every one of your examining staff, and the routes they work, the same in basic principle?

G. E.: Answering the last part of your question first—yes, we have a unified policy as regards our 23 Examiners and our 69 test routes throughout England, Scotland, Wales and Northern Ireland. Also, I would mention that each of our Examiners is required to be a thoroughly qualified ex-mobile Police driver who holds the Class I certificate, which, as you know, is the highest qualification that the official driving schools in which Police drivers have to spend many weeks in training can award. It also means they can handle any make and model of car to a standard of perfection few could excel, but every Examiner has further special training after joining the I.A.M. Each man has spent a good many years in the Police, and is now solely employed by the Institute. Do not, however, think of them as still being Police officers (I heard someone say the other day that the I.A.M. was run by the Police, which it most definitely is not). They are men hand-picked for their courtesy and tolerance towards our candidates. At the same time, they are firm in their judgment of driving ability and, if they do have to fail a candidate, tell him exactly why.

Now, as to what they look for when testing. They expect to be taken round the 35 mile route in good time, yet smoothly and safely. They rate dawdling as a defect just as much as brashness. Smoothness in handling clutch and gears, accuracy in positioning the car for taking bends and corners, also in traffic, is looked for, and avoidance of weaving from lane to lane, yet not obstructing faster vehicles. So is showing natural courtesy and consideration (but not an exaggeration of those qualities); making allowances for the misbehaviour of others, whether on foot or on wheels; not driving 'up the exhaust pipe' of the car ahead, but leaving a safe distance between. Not braking late or fiercely. Above all, not indulging in 'clever stuff', such as scalded-cat starts or overtaking with bare inches to spare. In short, demonstrating genuine understanding of how to behave towards other road users, passengers, and car.

C. E. : You mentioned smoothness in handling the car. Do you insist on a driver double de-clutching whenever he changes to a lower gear? I understand that the Police do in fact require this of their own men.

G. E. : Today, when almost every gearbox has synchromesh, or even automatic transmission, gear-changes do not call for the same techniques they necessarily did in the old days. As I said, however, we do ask that a driver should go from one gear to another with smoothness, balancing engine revs. with road speed. The engine should not be raced unduly during the change—it is quite unnecessary and may even militate against making a smooth change. And, of course, when synchromesh is not fitted to bottom gear it is essential to double de-clutch when engaging that ratio with the car on the move. We do expect a driver to be able to change down through all gears and into bottom with the car in motion. If he were at some time faced with a steep downhill and a failed brake, the safety of himself and his passengers, to say nothing of other road users, might depend on his being able to get into bottom gear. Naturally, we expect this change down to be made only while the car is travelling at a slow speed.

C. E.: Do you, therefore, regard the gearbox as an alternative to the brakes under normal conditions? If, for example, you were approaching a hazard where there would have to be some slowing of the car in order to negotiate it safely, would you consider it satisfactory to make a quick change down instead of applying the brakes?

G. E.: This depends on the car itself and the speed at which it is travelling. If it had a 3-speed box with a lowish middle gear and was travelling at a fast rate, the engine might be 'murdered' by changing down; we would think it showed lack of car sympathy. On the other hand, an E-type Jag, say, would be quite happy if you changed down to 3rd at 80. The chief reason we like the brakes to be used first when slowing is that it reveals whether they are in proper working order. Brakes do fail, we know, and it is better to be forewarned prior to an emergency arising. In fact, we endorse the drill the Police use when about to make a turn or round a sharp bend: it is easily remembered by the initials of the successive operations, namely C-M-S-B-G-A. They stand for Course (mentally selecting the correct position on the road for the manoeuvre), Mirror (checking on following traffic), Signal (as per Highway Code), Brake (to reduce speed and check brakes' working), Gear (changing down to the appropriate ratio), Horn (if desirable) and Accelerate (as soon as the driver considers it safe to do so, having regard to road conditions). Now, about signalling: we don't want a lot of superfluous hand flapping or flashing lights, first one side and then the other, making the car look like a Christmas tree. Another thing to remember is that the 'waving on' signal, which used to mean 'I am ready to be overtaken', is now officially obsolete—it savoured of being an instruction to a following driver, which is not permissible. All you can signal is your own intention, not attempt to drive the other man's car. But, if a signal would be likely to help the driver behind you, or an approaching one, then give it. Use trafficators always according to the circumstances prevailing at the time, with real meaning.

C. E.: You must have met with a wide variety of driving types in the course of your I.A.M. duties. I imagine that many people suffer from test nerves, yet are fundamentally thoroughly competent at the wheel, while no doubt there are equally some not so good who are all out to impress you with their personal ability?

G. E.: It has been my pleasure to go on test with many superb drivers of both sexes and all age groups. On the other hand, I have experienced both hair raising and exasperating drivers. Among the latter there is the type who seems determined to break all records for the course, and who completely disregards any Slow signs. I have been taken over X-roads at speeds above 30 m.p.h., and when I have pointed out the danger have been told 'So what? There was nothing coming—what's all the fuss about?'

C. E.: I suppose you receive a lot of letters from disgruntled candidates who have failed?

G. E.: Yes, and often they come from perfectly 'nice' people who start off by telling me that they have driven more than a million miles in everything from an Austin 7 to a tank transporter. They go on 'Your examiner told me that I should have driven faster and that I give too many signals. So you are trying to encourage dangerously high speed? And, even if your examiner trusts his mirror, I don't. And as for that nonsense about positioning, the correct part of the road is the near side—always. He also told me that I missed several warning signs—let me tell him that a good driver looks straight ahead and not sideways ...' And so on, sometimes for eight or ten pages.

Needless to say, these people are in the minority, and are far outnumbered by the large majority of candidates, both young and old, amateur and professional, whose attitude towards both driving and road safety leaves little to be desired. Even if some have not attained the standard we look for in members of the Institute, at least they learn something from their test, and usually come back for another 'go' when they have remedied the defects that were pointed out to them by our examiners. Indeed, I have sheaves of letters from people who both praise the manner in which their test was conducted and the helpful way the examiner afterwards advised them, no matter whether they passed or failed, on any driving points that needed improvement.

C. E.: Can we say, then, that the Institute regards as an advanced driver one who handles his car well and safely, neither dawdles nor dashes about, is mindful of others who have as much right to use the road as he has, gives proper signals when they would be helpful to following or approaching drivers, and pays full regard to warning signs erected for his guidance?

G. E.: Quite! And all I can add is that every action on the part of a really good driver is smooth and purposeful, his driving is decisive, well planned and carried out, and his passengers are never frightened that he will take an unjustifiable risk.

XXVIII

SUMMING UP

A CONSIDERABLE number of books have been written on the subject of good driving, but nevertheless many candidates have failed their Advanced test as a result of not **interpreting** their real meaning intelligently.

Thus, a manoeuvre which is perfectly safe today may be extremely dangerous tomorrow, or even at a later hour today. For example, you may be following a good driver along a stretch of road where it is perfectly safe to overtake—and you do so without the slightest qualm.

Tomorrow, on the other hand, you might be following a driver on the same stretch of road whose conduct causes you to mistrust him. Maybe he is chatting with his passengers and looking at them, or he may be slumped in his seat, elbow resting on door ledge and perhaps a couple of fingers holding the steering wheel.

Vehicles which carry the scars of 'prangs' are seldom the victims of others **every** time. Beware therefore the battered car or van whose driver is of the type mentioned above—exercise restraint and wait for the most favourable road conditions before attempting to overtake, and then give audible warning of your intention.

Weather and road conditions may also be such as to cause you to be wary and keep your speed moderated, also the distance you stay behind the vehicle ahead. If some ill-mannered driver crashes into the space you leave, drop further back.

It cannot be emphasised too strongly that really advanced driving means not only driving according to prevailing conditions of road, weather and traffic—it also means driving **defensively.** There are all too many louts on the road who have no thought but to press on regardless. Don't get involved with them.

Your own physical and mental condition likewise enters into the matter. If you are suffering from fatigue, a heavy cold or when worried or angry it would be wiser to use alternative means of transport. If you do decide to drive, however, pay attention to your physical or mental state, and drive accordingly. After a long and tiring day, drive home with even more care than usual, and slower if you are normally a reasonably fast driver. An advanced driver keeps calm and takes every precaution to avoid an accident or an 'incident', however much he is provoked.

Take nothing for granted and never assume that any other road user will do the right thing. Trust only your own skill and judgment.

There is a difference between being a 'good **driver**' and a 'good **motorist**'. The latter is of necessity a good driver, because he knows that 'attitude' and 'aptitude' are of equal importance.

However, there are many *technically* good drivers—able to clear narrow gaps at high speeds, make a car do a spin turn, carry out clutchless gearchanges—yet, despite their skill, are shockingly bad *motorists* as a result of their attitude to the subject.

The moment they get behind the wheel of a car they are obsessed with the power under their foot. Everybody else on the road is in their way—nothing must be ahead of them if it moves.

The **'good motorist'** goes on his way serenely and with courtesy towards others. He would never, for instance, 'blind' through a puddle if it meant saturating a passing pedestrian or cyclist.

None of us can claim never to have made a mistake, but we need not take unnecessary risks. All too frequently we hear the phrase 'I was in the right'. But who wants to be dead right? **Finally, remember, 'Driving is a state of mind'.**

XXIX

BRITISH TRAFFIC SIGNS

THE new type British signs are gradually taking over as this issue goes to press, but it will be some time before all of the old type are replaced. Drivers must, however, familiarise themselves with the new ones, and on following pages we illustrate many of them and describe their meaning.

Categories 1–4 give definitions as follows:

1. REGULATORY SIGNS are circular (except the Stop and the Give Way signs). Prohibitory signs have a wide red border and most mandatory ones have a blue background. A white rectangular plate below a sign amplifies its message.

2. WARNING SIGNS are mostly triangular, point uppermost, having a wide red border. As with regulatory signs, a plate may amplify the message.

3. DIRECTION SIGNS are rectangular but may have a pointed end where they show the place at which the driver should turn. Signs on motorways have a *blue* background, on primary routes a *green* ground, and on other routes a *white* ground. Signs with a wide *blue border* show directions to local places.

4. INFORMATION SIGNS, also rectangular, generally have a blue ground.

1. Regulatory signs, generally speaking, render the driver liable to a penalty for failing to obey them. In addition to speed limits, Stop, Give Way, prohibitions as to weight and size of vehicles, waiting and parking, overtaking, etc., they include No stopping ('Clearway'), 'Play Streets', No right (or left, or 'U') turn and No entry for all or certain types of

vehicle. These include the 'STOP' sign containing an inverted triangle which instructs a driver that he MUST stop (viz. bring his vehicle to an absolute stop) at the main road immediately ahead, AND that he must then give way to any traffic on that road; also the inverted triangular 'GIVE WAY' sign which means 'yield priority to traffic on such main road without necessarily stopping dead'.

2. Warning signs do not carry specific penalties, but failure to obey them or take heed could well lead to, or strengthen a charge for driving without due care and consideration. There can be little or no excuse for becoming dangerously involved at a road hazard if you have been given advance warning of its presence by one of these signs.

The 'School' sign comes under this heading, and should always be treated with respect, especially at times children are likely to be going to school or leaving at midday and evening. So should signs which give warning of possible slippery roads and the numerous other hazards which are here illustrated.

Traffic signs in Britain should not be considered as being identical with those in use abroad. It is true to say that some are very similar, but others are quite different, and in any case there is no complete agreement between all countries as to their national signs even though basically they may be uniform (and in many cases comparable with the new British ones). As, however, this Manual is intended for drivers in Britain, we have not attempted to include their foreign counterparts.

In addition to roadside signs, there are road surface markings. They denote the following:

(a) Single solid white line across left-hand carriageway: stop line at signals or police control.

(b) Twin solid white lines across left-hand carriageway: stop lines at Stop sign.

(c) Twin broken white line across carriageway: 'Give Way' signal.

(d) 'V' sign painted on carriageway: warning of 'Give Way' sign.

(*e*) Double white lines (both solid or one solid and one broken): not to be crossed or straddled by a vehicle which has a solid line on its offside nearest the driver. Stopping is prohibited where the lines are laid.

(*f*) Broken white line, widely spaced: lane guide.

(*g*) Ditto, less widely spaced: centre line of carriageway.

(*h*) Broken white line with long sections interspersed by short gaps: warning line of impending hazard.

There are also yellow markings (mainly in congested streets) to denote waiting and/or loading restrictions, the exact times of which are shown on nearby plates (or at the entries to controlled parking zones); but the pattern of the markings gives a general warning of the extent of the prohibitions—as follows:

Yellow lines alongside the kerb show where waiting (except for loading and unloading) is prohibited:

(*a*) Broken yellow line: periods less than every working day (e.g. daily peak periods, or longer periods on alternate days).

(*b*) Solid yellow line: the whole of every working day.

(*c*) Double solid yellow line: more than every working day (e.g. from early morning and/or to late at night, or at all times).

Short yellow lines (or '*dashes*') *across* the kerb show that loading and unloading is banned within times shown on plates, etc., as follows:

Single lines or dashes: as (*a*) above.

Twin lines or dashes: as (*b*) above.

Treble lines or dashes: as (*c*) above.

XXX

FOR ALL MOTORISTS

'EVERYONE is presumed to know the Law' runs a well-worn legal axiom: 'Ignorance is no excuse' says another. One Member of Parliament has hazarded in the House of Commons that there are more than 2,000 regulations which concern the motorist, and whatever the total may be the fact remains that some £8 million a year is collected annually from the motoring population in fines, quite apart from parking tickets.

It is almost inevitable that, at some time or other, a police officer will have occasion to speak to a motorist about an alleged breach of the Law. It behoves a driver on such encounters to respond in such manner as to make it possible for the officer to warn instead of reporting, if the former course lies within his discretion. To adopt a recalcitrant attitude, or to deny the alleged offence out of hand, obviously puts a warning out of the question. If the officers considers that his duty is to report, he will invariably enquire whether an explanation can be tendered and record this in his notebook. Even if the explanation depends on facts which are later brought to mind, a letter should be sent with the least possible delay to the Police of the area concerned setting these facts forth clearly and concisely in the hope that a caution and not a summons will ensue.

For the purposes of the Road Traffic Act, the term 'road' signifies 'any highway or other road to which the public has access and includes bridges over which a road passes.' A road covers the verge and pavement adjoining the carriageway. Any offence connected with lights must occur on a 'road' within this meaning: so far as vehicle taxation and registration are concerned an offence must take place on a 'road repairable at public expense', i.e., an 'unadopted' road does not count. Now, so far as lighting is concerned, not every motorist realises that his head, side and tail lamps must be in full working order *by day* as well as after dark. Also that headlamps must be kept on (dipped or full beam) when travelling on an *unlit* road, including motorways. Further, that it is an offence to leave the headlamps on when the car is stationary; that during the hours of darkness a car must not be parked without lights at a less distance than 15 yards from a road junction; or (in the London district) on any bus route. Or that flashing lights must not be used except on 'authorised' vehicles (fire engines, police cars, ambulances, etc.); or that sidelamps must be at least 2 feet from the ground, have bulbs of not more than 7 watts consumption, and have the wattage indelibly marked on them. In addition, that light other than dipping headlamps may not be moved by swivelling, as in the case of a spotlamp, but that the beam of light from not more than two front lamps (not obligatory lamps) may turn in conjunction with the front wheels if the centre of the lamps is not more than $3\frac{1}{2}$ feet from the ground. The current Highway Code deals specifically with road markings ('Lines and Lanes', page 11) and illustrates several but not one which is becoming more used (para. 54), namely, a special form of double white line in which the lines are separated by an area marked with diagonal lines. This is found on road humps and dips and separates opposing streams of traffic by a safety gap. It also, as the Highway Code states, protects traffic turning right. Vehicles should not be driven over the diagonal lines 'if you can avoid doing so', while for traffic going straight ahead it must be regarded as the equivalent of the double white line.

Finally, every motorist should acquaint himself thoroughly with the warning signals now being used on Motorways, both rural and urban. On the latter the signals are displayed on gantries above the traffic lanes, and give instructions as to maximum speed advised, or to stop and wait a signal to proceed. Warning of a closed lane, danger or accident ahead, lane to be used—all these signals MUST BE OBEYED and hence must be clearly understood. On urban motorways the signals are on the central reserve, at 2-mile intervals.

British Traffic Signs

Warning signs

Distance to
STOP sign
ahead

Cross roads

Roundabout

T junction

Staggered
junction

Distance to
GIVE WAY
sign ahead

Side road

Plate below
some signs

Sharp deviation
of route to left
(or right if
chevrons reversed)

Bend to right
(or left if symbol reversed)

 Double bend
first to left
(may be reversed)

 Series of
bends

 Two-way traffic
straight ahead

 Two-way traffic
crosses
one-way road

 Traffic merges
from left

Traffic joins
from right

 Road narrows on
offside (nearside if
symbol reversed)

 Road narrows
on both sides

 Dual carriageway
ends

 Steep hill
downwards

 Steep hill
upwards

 Children

109

Single file in
each direction

Pedestrian
crossing

Traffic
signals

Hump bridge

Uneven road

Plate with
CHILDREN sign
at a school

Road wide enough
for only one line
of traffic

Road works

Change to opposite
carriageway
(may be reversed)

Right-hand lane
closed (symbols
may be varied)

Slippery road

Plate with
CHILDREN sign
near school
crossing patrol

Level crossing
with automatic
half-barriers
ahead

Level crossing
with other
barrier or
gate ahead

Level crossing
without gate or
barrier ahead

Location of
level crossing without
gate or barrier

'Count-down' markers
approaching concealed
level crossing

Height limit
(e.g. low bridge)

Available width of headroom
indicated

Opening or
swing bridge

Quayside or
river bank

Overhead electric
cable; plate
indicates maximum
safe height for
vehicles

Cattle

Wild animals

Horses or ponies

Worded warning
sign

Distance to
hazard

Falling or fallen
rocks

Low-flying
aircraft or sudden
aircraft noise

Distance over
which hazard
extends

Other danger;
plate indicates
nature of
danger

SIGNS GIVING ORDERS

Those with red circles— mostly prohibitive

Maximum speed limit

Maximum speed limit 70 mph

Stop and Give Way

Give way to traffic on major road

No entry

School Crossing Patrol

No waiting

No stopping ("Clearway")

No right turn

No left turn

No U turns

No overtaking

Give priority to vehicles from opposite direction

All motor vehicles prohibited (plate may qualify)

Buses and coaches prohibited

Lorries prohibited

No cycling or moped-riding

All vehicles prohibited (plate gives details)

Total weight limit

Axle weight limit

Width limit

Plate below sign at end of prohibition

No pedestrians

Blue circles with no red border—mostly compulsory

Minimum speed limit

End of minimum speed limit

Ahead only

Turn left (right if symbol reversed)

Turn left ahead (right if symbol reversed)

Keep left (right if symbol reversed)

Pass either side

Route for cyclists and moped riders (compulsory)

Plate supplementing 'Turn' signs

111

DIRECTION SIGNS

Direction to places reached by –

Direction to
a motorway

a primary route,

another route.

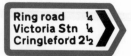

Direction and mileage
to local places

Best route for pedestrians

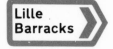

Direction to
Ministry of Defence
establishment

Route confirmatory sign

Ring
road

INFORMATION SIGNS

One-way traffic

One-way street

Priority over vehicles
from opposite
direction

No through
road

Advance warning
of no through
road

Hospital

Parking place;
plate indicates
lorry park

Entrance to
controlled
parking zone

Appropriate traffic lanes
at junction ahead

Direction and
distance to
public telephone

'Count-down' markers at exit from
motorway or primary route (each bar
represents 100 yards to the exit)

Direction to service area with fuel,
parking, cafeteria and restaurant facilities

Road
clear

Cyclists and
moped-riders
only

Weight limit
10 tons
3 miles
ahead

Dual
carriageway
ahead

ROAD MARKINGS

ACROSS THE CARRIAGEWAY

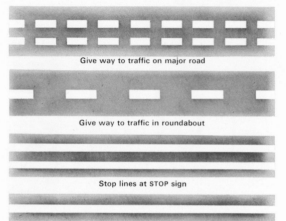

Give way to traffic on major road

Give way to traffic in roundabout

Stop lines at STOP sign

Stop line at signals or police control

Warning of Give Way sign

Box Junction See Rule 74

ALONG THE CARRIAGEWAY

Double white lines   Diagonal stripes   Lane markings

No crossing

No crossing solid line if nearer to driver than broken line

Do not enter marked area

Lane line   Centre line   Warning line

ALONG THE EDGE OF THE CARRIAGEWAY

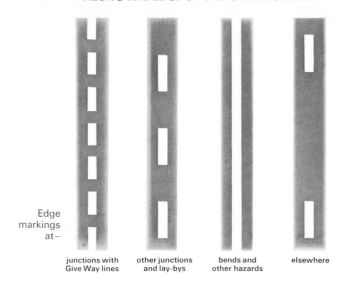

Edge markings at—

| junctions with Give Way lines | other junctions and lay-bys | bends and other hazards | elsewhere |

SCHOOL ENTRANCE

Keep entrance clear of stationary vehicles

No waiting (except for loading and unloading) at times shown on nearby plates or on entry signs to controlled parking zones

—during every working day*

—during every working day and additional times*

—during any other periods*

For example

Plate giving times

Continuous prohibition

Limited waiting

ON THE KERB OR AT EDGE OF CARRIAGEWAY

No loading or unloading at times shown on nearby plates

— during every working day*

For example

**No loading
Mon-Sat
8·30 am-6·30 pm**

— during every working
day and additional times*

For example

**No loading
at any time**

— during any
other periods

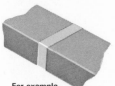

For example

**No loading
Mon-Fri
8·00-9·30 am
4·30-6·30 pm**

*May include Sundays (see plates)

Light signals

Pairs of alternately
flashing red lights side
by side mean
YOU MUST STOP

— at level crossings

— on urban motorways

Although illustrating a wide range of the new signs prescribed by the
Traffic Signs Regulations, The Highway Code does not show all variations.

ENVOI

This book would be incomplete without the provision of some background history and information about the Institute of Advanced Motorists.

The Institute has as its twin objectives the raising of driving standards and the promotion of road safety, the basic theory being that a road or a motor vehicle is just as safe or as dangerous as its driver. By improving his or her competence, a 'defensive' technique will be acquired which should enable him or her to cope safely with all situations that may arise while driving.

Initial proof of this theory was found in the dramatic reduction in accidents among Metropolitan Police drivers between the years 1935 and 1954, following the introduction of Approved Police Driving Schools in 1935. Figures produced by the Home Office showed that the use of advanced driving techniques in the Metropolitan Police had reduced accidents to one-sixth of their previous total.

In a public speech in November 1954 the then Minister of Transport, Mr. John Boyd Carpenter, suggested that an 'Honours Degree' for motorists could be an aid to road safety. A standard of driving should be set, he proposed, which the novice could seek to attain, and which motorists of long-standing should have reached. An Advanced Driving Test would reveal faults and should indicate their cure.

This advice was acted upon and a Steering Committee under the Chairmanship of the late Lord Sempill, A.F.C., after long and careful consideration, brought the Institute of Advanced Motorists into existence in March 1956. It is a non-profit-earning Company, limited by guarantee, and governed by a

Council on which sit representatives of many important bodies and also several Members of Parliament.

The Council at that time appointed Mr. George Eyles, M.B.E., as Chief Examiner, placing in his experienced hands (he is himself the holder of a Class 1 Police Driving Certificate) the task of organising the I.A.M. Advanced Driving Test. The successful completion of this would constitute the 'Honours Degree' envisaged by the Minister and entitle the candidate to become a Member of the Institute.

Before testing actually began, three major steps were taken: firstly a standard of driving had to be set, and this was worked out in collaboration with the Ministry of Transport, and based upon the well-tried and proven Police system. Secondly, test routes had to be selected in different parts of the country, each to be comparative one with another so as to ensure to the maximum extent similar conditions for everyone taking the Test. It was considered that the duration must be at least $1\frac{1}{2}$ hours and that city streets, derestricted highways and winding country lanes must be included.

Finally, the selection of Examiners had to be made, and this involved taking a decision upon which the whole success of the Institute in the field might depend. The Examiners must obviously be experts and seen to be such; hence the choice fell upon ex-Mobile Police Officers holding a Class 1 Police driving certificate. To gain this a man must receive long and comprehensive training, both theoretical and practical, followed by years of driving experience under all conditions, including emergencies. As it was also highly important that a candidate should be put at ease right from the start of his voluntary Test, the Examiners must be chosen with an eye on their ability to deal with people in the right manner. Each Examiner was therefore selected with very great care and it is pleasing to report that many candidates—even those who failed in the Test—have written in to express their appreciation of the courtesy and painstaking work of their Examiner and the valuable advice they received from him at the conclusion of their Test.

The Institute's first Tests started in June 1956 and, apart from a setback during the period of the Suez crisis when petrol was rationed, has gone steadily and successfully forward. In the first ten years 108,289 Tests were conducted, from which 60,338 Members were admitted.

An important development had during this time taken place, insofar as commercial firms were beginning to realise the advantages of entering their driving staff for the Test. Where such firms paid the Institute's fee, a written report was sent to a named person in the Management. Experiences reported by such firms has made it apparent that, by taking this step, costs resulting from bad accident records could be cut.

During 1957 I.A.M. Members in Nottingham conceived the formation of a 'Group' for both social purposes and the promotion of road safety locally. The idea caught on and, at the time of going to press, 40 similar Groups have come into existence, purely through Members' own enterprise. They do much valuable work in various fields of endeavour, among which may be mentioned the serving by Members on local Road Safety Committees and co-operation with the Ministry of Health in the training of disabled drivers who are provided with single-seater invalid cars. Out of the small fee paid by the Ministry for this service, some Groups have managed to amass sufficient sums to purchase a Guide Dog for the Blind.

Although it might be said that the Institute has barely reached the fringe of the many millions who hold driving licences, its Advanced Driving Test does seem to have made motorists at large realise that there *is* a higher standard of driving and road manners to be achieved. During the last four years advanced driving classes have been started by local authorities in cities and towns with the object of raising students' standards to the requirements of the I.A.M. Test. The Institute believes that Education is the long-term answer to the road accident problem and that, by its ten years of effort, has probably played a large part in generating the need for, and the target of, these classes.

In conclusion, the Institute hopes that it will build up in time a really vast body of skilful and responsible motorists—not just good drivers—who, by their personal example and encouragement of others to improve, will make the roads safer for all who use them.